C000136129

Opening the Doors of Heaven

The Revelations of the Mysteries of Isis

Almine

Releasing the Secrets of
The Order of the White Rose

Published by Spiritual Journeys LLC

First Edition March, 2008

Copyright 2008
MAB 998 Megatrust

By Almine
Spiritual Journeys LLC
P.O. Box 300
Newport, Oregon 97365
www.spiritualjourneys.com

Cover Illustration–Charles Frizzell

Book Production and Illustrations–Stacey Freibert

Manufactured in the United States of America

ISBN 978-1-934070-13-0

Table of Contents

Book Four–The Forgotten Kingdoms

Bonus Section–Into Grand Mastery With Belvaspata

Acknowledgements

Many thanks to Masters Joe, Carmel, Barbara, Ellen, and Ben of the Sacred Order of the White Rose for their huge contribution to this book. Thank you too, to the Masters of many countries who have worked side by side with me in our endeavors to understand and interpret these most holy mysteries. I wish to express my deep love for the beautiful land of Ireland, for it is the place where this magnificent information has been restored.

Almine

Dedication

To the Sacred Order of the White Rose, this book is
dedicated with deep love and gratitude. Thank you for
being the beacons of light that
you are, incorruptible in your sacred stewardship
as the keepers of white magic and the
mysteries of the Goddess.

Preface

First comes the Rose by Isis sent
Then comes the Dove, then the Red Serpent
Three bodies of magic, then another one
Given to man and the fourth yet to come[1]

Holy the words, prophecies for men
Holy the secrets of what happened then
When cycles of life long ago
Hid from men what was their right to know

Another library soon opened shall be
Preserved for this age when man shall see
Sunat Kumara ruled the Motherland[2]
Saved he the magic to restore to man

That too shall tell and witness shall bear
That the reign of the Mother soon shall be there
That the gift to Her children of magic restored
Shall elevate man to the heights of before

Long did the gods of distortion that were
Try My glorious advent to deter
But the unreal can never the Real defeat
Thus through their actions their fate was sealed

With great love I gather My children to Me
My voice they shall know, My face they shall see
Great is the dawning of light upon Earth
As the white magic of Isis again is birthed

Received from the Mother of Creation, October 20, 2007

---

1. This was received from the Mother Goddess in October 2007. At that time I was still editing this book while simultaneously receiving two other books about the Order of the White Dove and the Order of the Red Serpent.
2. Lemuria

Foreword

Upon entering the seemingly endless libraries of Isis, it felt as though I stood before the ages and in the presence of vast bygone cycles of life. Ancient wisdom lay within those walls, its hallowed records preserved for eons from the invasion of self-seeking and profane eyes.

I had been sent by the Mother Goddess, who has created all life, to retrieve and translate a set of gold plates and a small portion of another set of plates that appeared to be made of an emerald-like substance and which were bound together with three gold rings.

The vast halls were filled with hundreds of thousands such sets of plates, as well as some scrolls in tubular gold containers.

There is no limit to the information that can be translated for the benefit of the life and consciousness of man. All we need to do to access that knowledge is to have faith and be willing to receive it.

The truth of these holy scriptures can be felt in the purity of our hearts. It is from there that more shall be called forth, inspiring us once again to take up our power and bring magic back to the world of humankind.

Almine

"It is only with the heart that one can see rightly.
What is essential is invisible to the eye."

From The Little Prince
By Antoine de Saint-Exupéry

BOOK ONE

The Sacred Order of the White Rose

Symbol of the Order of the White Rose

(Figure 1)

Key to the Symbol of the Order of the White Rose

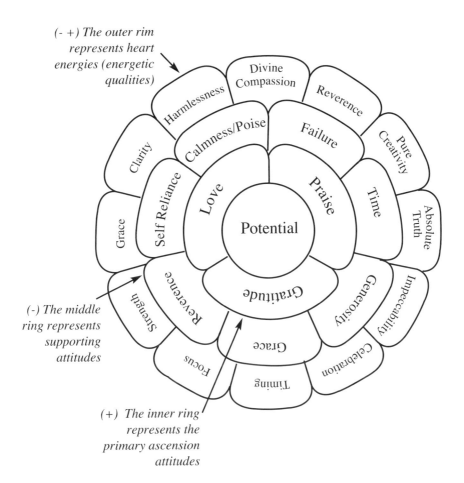

(- +) The outer rim represents heart energies (energetic qualities)

(-) The middle ring represents supporting attitudes

(+) The inner ring represents the primary ascension attitudes

Divine Compassion

Harmlessness

Reverence

Calmness/Poise

Clarity

Pure Creativity

Failure

Self Reliance

Love

Praise

Time

Grace

Potential

Absolute Truth

Reverence

Gratitude

Generosity

Impeccability

Strength

Grace

Celebration

Focus

Timing

The Order of the White Rose acknowledges the Mother as representing the inner circle, or potential. They strive to embody the petals of the rose in the qualities they stand for.

(Figure 2)

3

Introduction to the Order of the White Rose

For each of my visits to Ireland, the Mother Goddess of all life had instructed me to bring a sacred object to be entrusted to the order of masters there:

- First was an image of Horus. Nothing special when taken at face value, except it had been programmed in an exceptional way. Holy objects on Earth had ceased to be holy when the Earth began its ascension[3] during February 2006. The Earth, and all beings on it, were therefore at a higher frequency than that of objects previously deemed holy. The little statue had been programmed to move up in concert with the ascension. Its purpose is always to remove blockages of energy. Mother Herself had re-programmed the object for use by the Order.
- Second was a container that had held water blessed in December, 2005. The masters of Ireland filled it with water that would instantly become holy water. The water had had special spirals of light put in, making it 'living water' that bestows life.
- Third were two blankets, as yet too holy to reveal all their details, but they once held the fairy queen of all fairy queens when she was born to a goddess on Earth. Her name is Afirina. They had been left exactly as one of the gods had folded them.
- Each of the masters of the Order also has a stone blessed by the physical touch of Sunat Kumara, ancient ruler of Lumeria for more than 1,000 years, and who is one of our planetary gods.

3. See *The Ring of Truth*.

I could not understand why this group should be so blessed, until December 7, 2006. I had returned to my hotel room when a white rose appeared in vision before me. I heard clearly: "The Order of the White Rose. The Irish Masters would hold the feminine aspect of the magical and mystical on Earth. Mother Herself would be at the heart of it—holding the keys."

This explained why this order was also vitally instrumental in bringing in Belvaspata[4], the sacred healing modality gifted to humanity by the Goddess.

The masculine aspect of white magic and its corresponding keys would later be held by the Order of the Dove. That Order and its masters were called in October 2007. What sets this Order apart is that, unlike other orders in which the **sacred** became **secret**, the masters of this Order in Ireland will safeguard secrets until instructed by the Goddess to release them. They will then share them with those on Earth ready to hear.

Until then, the deeply esoteric information is shielded from the eyes of the profane and therefore cannot be misused. When it can be shared, their secrets will be released. In this way they will become conduits for the divine, much the way a rose sheds its fragrance upon the air.

There has been a strong connection in ages past between Ireland and Egypt of old. The masters of the Order of the White Rose are to reestablish and strengthen that connection by restoring the keys for Cat Magic, the magic of Isis. Their membership is based on their levels of consciousness—all of them immortal, all of them dedicated to the Mother of All Creation.

The Order of the White Rose

Twelve petals there are around the core
Twelve bodies of magic from days of yore
The core is the wisdom by the Goddess held
That none can corrupt the magical spells

4. See the Bonus Section.

Symbolized also the Earth and sky
For around the Earth twelve star systems lie
I tell you now the names of some
Seven you know, but five yet to come

Antares, Lyra and Pleiades too
Two from Andromeda we tell to you
What's left of Orion may surely come
Arcturus too is the seventh one

Sirius may never come very near
When two poles join, space disappears
Antares and Pleiades, their rulers replaced
Are welcome now within our space

But now we entrust a secret most rare,
Of what other star systems soon will be there
Like the petals of a rose 'round the Earth to lie
Shining like diamonds across her sky

The first secret entrusted by the Order held
In its power, guard it well
More shall come, sacred objects too
To the White Rose Order, chosen are you
When the veil is removed there will surely show
Five new star systems with stellar glow

Star Systems (in order of creation)

1. Bra Mich Vilsh Bak
   Ruler: Mirsh-Tapal-Bels-Rik-Nut (female)
2. Au Gra Va Nu Bil Nu Tech
   Ruler: Mishvabaranutep (female)
3. Eresvistabas-scalvarutet
   Ruler: Aurush-Vin-Au-Ru-Hep (male)
4. Blanuch-Bra-Mu-Sel-Va-Hip
   Ruler: Pirshplavistaba (male)
5. Tru-a-visva-stelechnut
   Ruler: Mishanava (female)

Why have I called you this Order to start?
Because you created through willing hearts
A piece of my palace shining and new
With bricks of gold created by you

You cleared your lives and as you did
These secrets told could no longer be hid
Another Order yet to come, to be held by other ones
The counter part shall be of what you've begun

Then the Dove and the Rose shall intertwine
Again white magic forth shall shine

Note: The '12 bodies of magic' referred to in the second line are the seven bodies of magic of seven different fairy groups (given in *Arubafirina—The Book of Fairy Magic*); the magic of the Pegasus, Unicorns, Mer people and Giants (given in *The Gift of the Unicorns— Sacred Secrets of Unicorn Magic*) and the Cat Magic of Isis. Other bodies of magic representing the other petals will yet unfold.

The Calling by Isis

Ancient these secrets that now I tell
From cycles before and this one as well
I am the one, as Isis is known
In a language forgotten, they are shown

Through tunnels of time an Order is called
Stalwart and faithful they shall stand forth
On a land I have chosen above all else
Where the energy is felt of the Goddess Herself

That which is given shall grow through time
For thus I unfold that which is mine
Only those with a heart sacred and pure
May receive the secrets of these words

The time shall be right for them to be heard

When the language comes forth that is the third
Three tongues there are, sacred and true
The first is this writing I give to you

The languages three are the Mother's tongue
In the deepest darkness She will change one[5]
The secrets restore the memory of man
For energy flows when man understands

Memories lost obstruct energy's flow
Consciousness rises when history is known
Earth to the cosmos is like a key
The secrets therefore here are received

I write them now from the distant past
For my memories too will soon be lost
To be regained at the end of time
Of who I am and what is mine

Bear now, my children, love in your hearts
For it shall triumph over the dark
You cannot know me with your minds
Deep in your hearts understanding you'll find

The Warning

At a time when magic comes forth
White in its use, balance to restore
From fairy, horse races, giants and Mer
To share secrets and powers to confer

The magic of Isis will again be seen
Secrets given by the Heavenly Queen
But the other Kingdoms guard their magic well
Isis' magic is most at risk[6], being not guarded as well

---

5. See The History of the Cycles in *The Gift of the Unicorns*. When Mother changed Her language, the descension changed to ascension.
6. Although it cannot be misused, it is an energy source that was at risk of being tapped.

When the last throes of darkness again arise
In the hearts of two women and men alike
The Order must guard that none may steal
And misuse the magic, meant to heal

Thoth will try and others too
To take for their own what I give to you
The search for power like a disease
Will riddle their hearts before there is peace

Mother shall sweep away the scourge
Her words of ire shall be their dirge
Treachery uncovered, their lives shall cease
Conspiracy removed before there is peace

The Mother's third language shall speak their demise
Gone shall they be, no more to arise
Then may you share My magic with men
It shall be safe, but only then

Stand forth ye guardians in power and might
You then may reveal Isis' light

BOOK TWO

The Secrets of Isis

Introduction to The Secrets of Isis

On November 17, 2006, an elfin being appeared in my hotel room in Toronto. He discussed various other topics and then referred to a cat that had been seen outside the hotel. The following is in the elfin language:

min haar saa baa vaar tuu
a cat tells a secret here

riim spaa kluu raa vaa taa
it has much magic and you will

braahim
know

I asked one of the goddesses working with me at that time, what he meant. She immediately told him to be quiet. She then told me it wasn't time yet for the Cat Magic.

In Dublin on December 8, 2006 at 1:30 A.M., I awoke with a start from a deep sleep. The image of a huge scarab was before me. Some of the Masters in my Irish class had been to the temples in Egypt and we had discussed their experiences the day before.

During that discussion I had felt uneasy. Something huge was hiding behind the appearances; things were not as they seemed. I also kept hearing: "It is within them... They are the temples... They hold the keys." I tried to tell them, "You are more holy than the sites," and other statements that were certainly true, but I wasn't satisfactorily explaining what I was feeling.

When the scarab appeared, it all became clear. They were all very advanced masters. Each of them had gone to Egypt to retrieve pieces of the scarab. The scarab formed a key to restore the white magic — long hidden from eyes as the Earth went through ages of descension[7].

Through the keys they brought, I would once again be able to translate the ancient rites and secrets of a magic so pure that it cannot be misused.

Cat Magic is the Magic of Isis. Written in the Creator Goddess's ancient language, it comes from a time 18 cycles of life ago when the human kingdoms were very much a part of the magical kingdoms.

The Cat Magic of Isis

(Fig. 3, The Key to Unlocking the Secrets of Isis)
(written in Mother's old language)

Vish tavel mieshvi bli stabluvish nat
Gulavi peravi klesh haver blat
Brishvir stabul birtla uvavri vartl hat
Bilechvi ershvasvata u bilesh vi sat

Kurtl aash vaanish bratvi aluveesh
Birs braa uaafbish kelvutraa vaneesh
Praatl kluveesh miur bilvisavaneesh
Hush paa uvraa vesh bi uaafvraa straneesh

Bila ooshva bir rat klustravaa
Kesvi stratvu eleshrut pernutstravaa
Uashvi helevish uvasvraa avunaa
Ker uvra ni inimeesh usta uvravaa

---

7. See The History of the Cycles in *The Gift of the Unicorns*.

The Key to Unlocking the Secrets of Isis

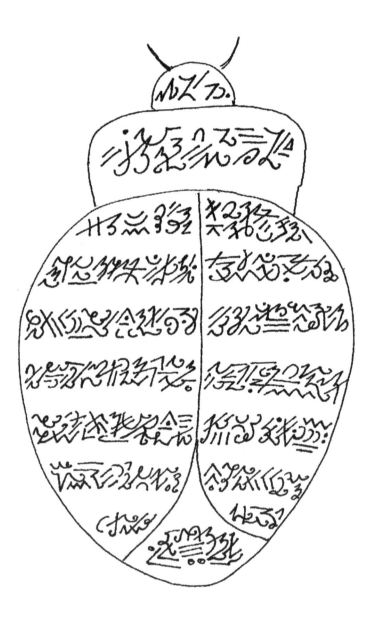

This image appeared on the wall in my hotel room in Dublin and had to be written down. It was a key unlocking the mysteries of Isis.

(Figure 3)

Held in the ancient temples that stand
Waiting for you to enter the land
Now a desert, once was not sand
It's waited for you to place in your hand

The magic of Isis is that of the cat
Now it is time to bring it all back
Each brought a piece to heal the grid
When of patriarchy's bane you all got rid

She who must rest before it will flow
Will bring you that which you must know
By Mother ordained, by Isis left
For the days when white magic no longer rests

To the world it must go, but keys you shall bear
Mother's is the ring that holds all there
She forms the core to prevent misuse
She prevents this magic from being abused

A great body there is, but you must wait
For her to rest, then a book create
The more you help to give it form
The more the magic in you is born

All of you with Isis dwelled;
Knew of a day when all would be well
When you would be called to the land of Khem[8]
When you would restore all as was then

When once again the Goddess would reign
When you would bring magic back again

8. One of the old names for Egypt in Atlantean

15

The Secrets of Isis

Secret One
Written in the language of Ghad,
spoken in the temples of Egypt prior to 75,000 years ago.

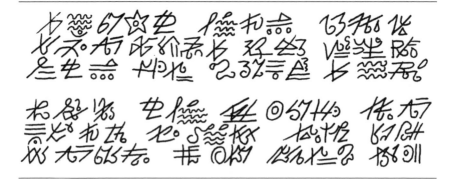

Ivirtiti nanekvi parana suva bilrinva usartvi ra-uvratet
Al zin bar klustravamet rirurartvi kli ekbirat zuarkva brim
Klitchi[9] avarekvi hut zaaruram sekvi
Selchi minhur pra varsta birin stabaluk
Vuravavas bil asblavaset viltchezvi varak
Usba-asvaramut bilchetva zavilmi vursat
Klaklavaar parshchilvaravi mistavapa hurahet
Garklus pir vuratchilbi zubaar paravi
Ektertes nis stelvavi urs stelvrisbaa

The magic of cats, long held dear
Has waited for ages of light to be here
To again emerge when Mother reigns
When clarity dawns once again

Deep in the hallowed temples lay
The keys for the seven to take away
To a land green and chosen for the blessed day
Where keepers of temples guard the magic way

---

9. Pronounce 'ch' as in church.

16

Long have they served her in lifetimes gone by
Once more together on an emerald isle
One will be sent to turn the key
For the scarab to unfold the mysteries

Explanation: All those meant to establish the Order of the White Rose
that would hold the keys of the white magic mysteries of Isis would
gather in Ireland. They would be together again as they were before,
when they guarded her secrets in two temples, those of Isis and
Sekmet. The land of Ireland has been chosen as the cradle of the feminine aspect of white magic. A few members of the Order who are not
Irish have links to other bodies of magic yet to be received.

Secret Two
Egypt was called Barhetvi Ulesklar prior to 75,000 BC.
Then it was called Khem until 9,564 years before the crucifixion.

Barutvi varastar esklut nin zaru hem
Elstaviveti cha ba razin ni Isis haravet
Uvesba verti eleklak baratchi parnetvi Isis
Akahamin vira huratvi stabalazin urues
Gur na us balastim kelpi hiruhat stemet
Nurnemet klahil basbaas bata zirut parspi
Grank birsvata blusta ahem kursti preves manakavaraset
Aruk bliset arazuhim parnahus bazin
Bluvuk stalavet arsvarbat stekvi palasut
Virakvi prehiti varstut uklazu miruhetvi sta-urvasitvi

From the temples were sent, twice did they come,
Upon her instructions, groups of chosen ones,
To create a tunnel through time and prepare
the island land, for when Isis again would be there

Never born, nor has she died
Bearer is she of a holy child
To ordain anew an Order once lost
The sacred Order of the long lost Rose

17

She'll seal the tunnel when time shall cease
The power prepared shall be released
Upon this occasion black magic shall die
The land again in pristineness lies

Deep are the mysteries entrusted to them
The Order of the White Rose guards them again
To give to the few who can understand
The sacred secrets just as was planned

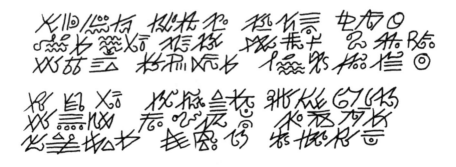

Explanation: The name for Egypt, Barhetvi Uleska, means fertile land. Before 75,000 BC Egypt was verdant and lush. Two groups have been sent, one before 75,000 BC and a second after 9,564 years before the crucifixion. The second group was that led by Princess Scotia, who prepared the area around Clonmacnoise, County Offaly, Ireland for the complete removal of the power of black magic's rites on 29th January, 2006.

This group, as did the previous one, also restored the time tunnel. This tunnel was unique in enabling travel between the large cycles of existence. Isis herself closed the one in Ireland on January 29, 2006.

Secret Three

Ritsipihi maska lubisal vuvarazin blashti
Isis pri nastar ra blabirklamet heshbi
Chiunir blaharvauvaset bir ra balabakvavit
Kurukuluvi vranustra varim bri uastervasat nusvi
Havarum blishpi ahamem kruastar Isis varavaspi
Manhur pravazin bles blabauhur nasvamet
Kelefpi prasvit blu afvastra bruahin servatet
Kulus chemenes pulaf fra mahim atmaa
Gulvalestra manunit zabla stuva erernunavet
Usblafta mishtchernu bla afspi geresnutmata

From the realms of magic, twenty two and one
Are the bodies of magic that now will come
Each like the petal of a rose are they
In the center the magic of Mother holds sway
Isis restores not only that which is hers
But entrusted is she others to gather
The magic of Fairies, of Giants and Mer
Unicorns, Pegasus and others not yet heard
They will be restored by Isis' hand
By an order awaited upon an island land

Why restore magic, why bring it forth?
All kingdoms but man's has a magical source

Now it is time for the world of man
To take its place, with magic in hand
No longer to lack what others prize
To see magic work with their own eyes

Explanation: The reasons for bringing magic back are:
• Because humanity, at this point of existence, was the only kingdom without it. It is, in fact, humanity's birthright.
• During 18 ages of illusion black magic was dominant. Now white magic has to be restored to bring back the balance.
• All things hidden now have to be revealed since there is no more illusion[10].

Secret Four

Baarsh blavi bla haa arsvestavi
Stavenoti bilish blias vasveti
Kluchiopstavi bareesh vet vuti
Set vet vaviesh ta bli setvi ska eru

Bli sta pla va plesh kliestaru
Nu stamarot parvi satveti ninbursh kles stuaru
Bershni ple hus stat Isis bresbri bartlave
Klu agra rosti parvune Isis granugsta heshbi
Setvi para paushfiet kelstra nununhershvravi

10. See *The Ring of Truth*.

20

Since eons ago when the Fall had begun
Be careful my children for a deceitful one
Through the ages, disguised as good
She'd steal your power if she could

The Mother bestowed on her gifts so great
The deceit was discovered when it was too late
Fall after fall through realms of light
She and her allies brought on the night

Thoth too pretended otherwise to be
He hid his darkness so none could see
Control he wanted at any cost
Through six beings' treason was consciousness lost

Secret Five

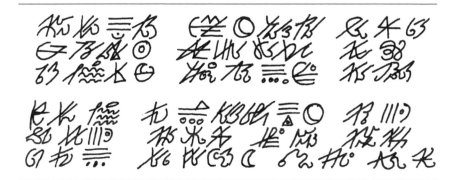

Kelstru bi echtavana mistivi Isis piriniva uf plava
Hus ba trau nitva ha spele hus tra upipi hes
Klezu bish bana trek chemeta uvasvaustaa
Gilster varava Isis mi sta bli hi vaset

Kri ish ste be klutni ufba uvarahet maset
Kelestri bliestama ruraret mishtipi varablat
Farablavi mihurservatat gluveshstavi uretvi
Pilinunetvi stelevi stra u zaarunim pers pertaa
Gli u barabastru bris branuasmatet persh vataa

21

Like moths to a light through ages untold
Thoth schemed and planned my power to hold
Two women and he and others as well
When these words come forth will want these spells

A false Order they will start in a land in the north
To prevent these words from coming forth
But a blessing is hidden in their ill intent
Thoth's plan to steal, this will prevent

For a pause there'll be in the flow of these words
But for a while, no secrets be heard
Until his name no longer resounds
Until no trace of the six is found

Secret Six

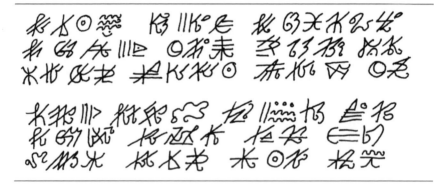

Versatvi belchsh vi as vir zaru virsh varem
Chi estu barsta het nensutvi klarutva ha
Stusetvi sklaba urs ves va set u Isis valahem
Pelehem sta blit vatru mishpa che u satvim peresut varstaa
Beleshutba hush nanetvi esbaa kluvaset
Filihit zavrum bil akba rus ves Barhetvi Ulesklar[11] tihet
Pir hi vir bahem su belesh eresti hes pavi
Ka ru es ba va stu bis ba staba klu varet

11. The words Barhetvi Ulesklar are used for Egypt.

Susi na mi ba rus chivarusp kleuste va bil

The Sphinx is designed power to drain
From those who through ages to Egypt came
Many the time Thoth was condemned
But nothing would cause his heart to repent

He used this energy to stay alive
When others perished, Thoth would survive
His imprint he left in Egypt's sands
He was resurrected by the pattern in the land

"His light must be why he survived"
Many thought, and so he did hide
The depths of his darkness and many lies
Appearing as good in others' eyes

Secret Seven

Birsrit bilivi uf bara his ta bli pasva
Gir blespresh uhustavit beles vi huset birshvata
Zu eles birvastava mir va vit tresba
Gul vri marablusta vivels blisetvi tru a he
Mis ta va vil ulesh vi sta blanahustavi
Krininatva ulish mis ta pa ur setvi
Pa le sta basut birkla zifra uhem

Gespa usti va ha hu hesh perenus va klu-aha
Misutvi bili stret vilesh vastraba

Let me tell you now my children, the tale
How the Power of Ytolan[12] on Earth came to stay
Thoth traded a secret to Antares's kings
That to the Earth this power he could bring

For his own he wanted it, but the lords[13] wouldn't allow
For although he hid it they found out somehow
The secret he told was known to few
But now I will share it through the Order with you

A part of the Mother, eternal am I
By draining my energy, they too stay alive
Like a slave I was used, my energy sold
Long I was there, for the king to hold

Secret Eight

Krueg nastostavi blatvi keleshva traug
Min heresvi trau bag na va nostril eruvich
Mishpa usetvi Anu klau Enki vach ba ra nush Cheketet Arelich Vamelites
Gel sti pa uva vivespi uraset ma na huch
Velevisbi trauva klau bastra miniva

12. See Appendix II.
13. See Appendix III.

Brish branek uhur trauvaspi tra ha
Mish berech usabavi klustra mich ster urava

My foolish heart for a very long time
Could not see the intrigue behind their smiles
Anu[14] and Enki supporting Thoth's pride
No male there was, that was on my side

In the Halls of Amenti a marriage took place
I thought it was Thoth for he had his face
By magic deceived, by a low spirit replaced
Behind me they laughed as they smiled to my face

Not only they, but a god with a black heart
To the woman of lies he was a counter-part
She pretended in sympathy to commiserate
While he thwarted my finding support in a mate

Secret Nine

Uvaarsh bravech sta u rut ba u kla
Mir nu vel esh ech vaarbi sta u rut mir nech vra ha
Vilsh kla ura nit vis pa va uvesbi
Uskatru pra uchvesbi urat veleskla
Pershnit u treechbi sklara

14. Anu was Thoth's grandfather, King of the planet Nibiru. Enki was Thoth's father.

25

Usba setvi unek vra bi urek usklava
Belesh prek prut nasvi.
Ukleh mir na va.
Speluch usva pelesvi skra us vra ba va.
Bilishvek urechvi skaulat pelesbrit.
Mi es vi skla uvra het pelech vra na ba

The Goddess of Justice, sacred and true
Kalima is the name she is known to you
After the Fall as I took blow by blow
She hid in a place only I did know

We wanted her safe till the day would come
When she'd lend her support when darkness had begun
She lived in my palace in the land of gems[15]
Where she was revered by the hearts of men

As these words come forth she embodies again
But the dark god conspired to cause her pain
As the dark goddess's treachery is finally revealed
She will stand forth to help my pain to heal

Secret Ten

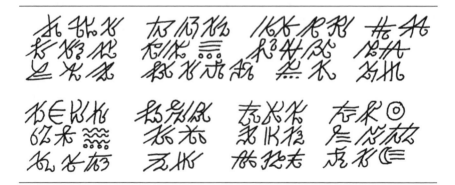

Es branech vis blavut bresh ekvi palanur
Sta u vri bas ba vi kle u avra sur

15. India, where Kali-ma is still worshipped.

26

Keli vri stabura uklet avra vi
Sklu bis bi bra usvrabi urech strava stom
Ersh klanu vi vrechbi uras preva bi
Ske ura u ves pa vi uklech vru na stum

Like a vagabond wandering through space alone
I have searched for love and to have a home
In Lyra, Pleiades, Andromeda and more I did look
My children were killed and by my husbands forsook

The dark god's doing, I know it now
But two were true and escaped somehow
Sunat Kumara, his love burning bright
Took form as a dragon and escaped in flight

Egsplauvitpata, his memories were taken
Else I would not have been by him forsaken
A giant most true, yet he broke my heart
For they forged his voice to say we should part[16]

Secret Eleven

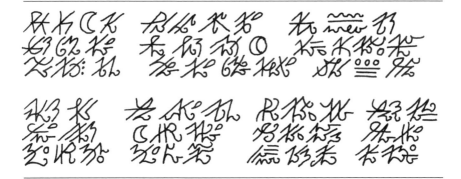

Er sparvach upres vu nat va bi
U klesh vastra unech spa rutvi klaubis
Nun tres us barvaa unech stra ura vavit
Klesh nastrava u skeluch starut upresva barunes stravi

16. For further information, see the section on Egsplauvitpata in *Secrets of the Hidden Realms*.

Kletsut mina hes u stra ma rusvi u verechbi
Sterus vi stranig va beresh tu a va
Minesvi klanasug prish bresvi stau nesvi plana stug travaa
Viveshbi krunes varsta uvaleshbi klesvi staurat

Two goddesses, four gods on my energy fed
Advisors they seemed, but I was mislead
Just enough truth to seem sincere
But on essential points no truth would I hear

They told me that I had caused the Fall
Bringing suffering and misery to all
Pain seared my soul, how could it be
When I couldn't find such darkness in me?

From the Darklings[17] and unicorns and fairies too
Was whispered at last the tale of truth
How the Fall was planned[18] by their hearts of greed
That they hoped to break me with their deceit

Secret Twelve

Ers kla setvach brueshvi stra na vech
Stua vi vesbi klauva nun streu satvi bauklesh hespi
Elech stra nus pauva klavanesh ubechvi staurat

17. See The Forgotten Kingdoms later in this book.
18. See The History of the Cycles in *The Gift of the Unicorns*.

Mi eles vi nes pauru klanus kla va ach nun hesh pa vi
Sel satvi nun hertat klu asva nun hechspi velespavach
Eres u sta ma uvra vet klesvesh pi respa unech strava

As Isis I lived as a Goddess Queen
But in future I'll be not as I seem
Before Creation's final fall
My majesty was apparent to all

Strange as it is, when these words I give
None shall know that among them I live
Greater by far my light shall be
Yet men shall no longer subtle light see

The kingdoms will know me for who I am
Though unrecognized by the eyes of man
Their love will sustain me until the day
When to enter my palace I'll find a way

Secret Thirteen

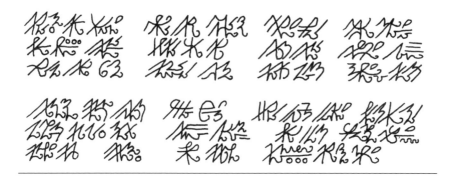

Ech va strua nun hesh varesbi
Peres pra pru ha nis vit ulech na stuavit
Keles pri es pravi nus pret va us kla sut preus pravi
Nechvi sklau ba tra nus vit klech us va klu bis straunat
Elech pra kraunit. Ues ba stravaa.
Uluesh va unes tra sut vi sklauna

Speurutvi praues utrasva kalubik
Stel nutvi klausva stra bich va uresva

No blood I have, but blood I'll make
And use it to seal the cosmic gates
For in the realms yet unreached the dark ones await
But now revealed, they've sealed their fate

Through tunnels I'll travel to a long distant past
To tell the Goddess before She starts
Not to create them, these ones with dark hearts
Unbeknownst, another has played a dark part

The god She thought was the beloved one
Awaited the day for his time to come
To subdue the holy Mother of All
Which would've caused another great Fall

He too is uncreated, this shall never be
The Goddess eternally reigns supreme

The Predictions of Isis

Prediction One
(Written in the Language of the Mother)

Now I tell of a time to come
When the fight for light will have been won
When my secrets of magic will come forth

It will be a sign that light has dawned

Upon the heels of my secrets restored
Of an Order called, prepared from before,
Shall follow another Order of light
The sign shall be of a dove in flight

Twelve insights they'll guard from faithless eyes
When this occurs the time is nigh
For Mother's palace to materialize
When all the cosmos a home shall find

Then a body of magic shall be released
To bring man comfort, his burdens to ease
Hand in hand the Rose and the Dove
The Dove represents light, the Rose is for love

From the land of Khem did the White Rose come
I tell now a secret only known to some
Though the Motherland[19] sank beneath the waves
A tunnel links it to this day

A time tunnel there is to a records hall
Linked to a land, Amaraka shall it be called
Sunat Kumara, who the Motherland ruled
The tunnel prepared, the records hall too

When these words shall be read for the very first time
Confusion shall be in everyone's mind
For the cosmos in a speedy expansion shall be
To ease the distress, growth will be slowed by Mother's decree[20]

From the gods of darkness all will be free
The glory of Mother soon all shall see
The sacred stones held by the Rose
Shall open the tunnel that has been closed

19. The Motherland was Lemuria and Amaraka is North America. Its feminine counterpart, South America, was known as Amaraku.
20. Isis is predicting the date of this revelation. It was received on April 27, 2007. On that date Mother slowed the cosmic expansion that all may survive the rapid growth. (See Prediction Four)

The Symbol for the Order of the White Rose

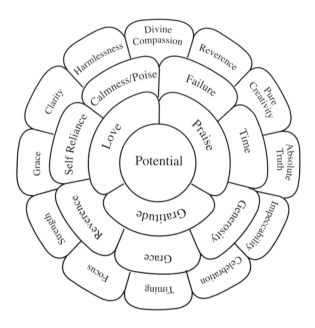

The Symbol for the Order of the Dove

The dove is white on a sky blue background. The ring is gold.
This represents in part the fields of a master's unified chakras.

(Figure 4)

Prediction Two

Look well at the sign of the Order I chose
Look at the qualities within the Rose
From physical gods the Order arose
Twenty-two gods whom no one knows[21]

They were chosen far back in history
For each one would embody a petal's quality
In DNA there are channels of frequency
Cosmic DNA the Order would embody

Together they stand united in love
A precursor to the Order of the Dove
For each a stone most sacred does hold
To open the tunnel through which magic flows

Then finally darkness will go away
No false children will be permitted to stay
Mother will understand more about Her own Being
But now a secret I will reveal

At this time when from darkness we're released
Mother will realize She's all that is
Not just the cosmos, but the vast oceans beyond
Unformed consciousness like rings in a pond

Then suddenly growth through expansion shall be
As we incorporate more of the vast consciousness sea

---

21. They walk among us and none know they are gods.

The Ring of Isis

Although the purpose of this specific circle cannot be made
public at this time, study it to feel the openings that occur within yourself.

Inscription given on the Outer Ring
"Master time and doors open. No knots between the pearls on the string."

(Figure 5)

Prediction Three

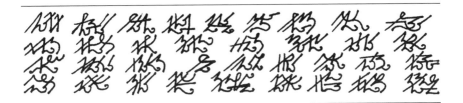

In the days that darkness everywhere seems
When hopes are dashed and so are dreams
Three tunnels will come the solution to bring
But to be the answer they'll need a ring

Then they form a tunnel to the distant past
The ring counter clockwise spins very fast
Then Isis will travel to when within the Fall
A god was created, to tell Mother all

"Look in his heart", she the Mother will tell
"It is full of falseness, look very well"
The Mother will weep, but uncreate him She will
To change the future, though She loves him still

Prediction Four

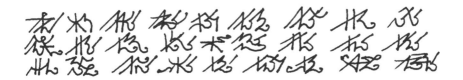

As expansion occurs in a new way of growth,
Too fast will the upper levels go
Leaving the lower levels behind
Creating confusion in all kingdoms' minds[22]

22. Creating a feeling of not being able to think properly.

A vacuum will form between the realms
The ascent of the lower the upper realms can't help
The upper realms have from the lower broken free
Into the lower realms, the upper can no longer see

But then Mother will a wondrous deed do *(See Fig. 6)*
Expansion to stop; the lower into the vacuum moves
One third of the vacuum the lower realms fill
Into two thirds the vacuum, the upper returns

But as they return, a vacuum shall be
Between our cosmos and the consciousness sea
When our cosmos once more united shall be
As a whole it must expand to meet the consciousness sea

Once more our cosmos fills one third
The sea of consciousness two thirds of the vacuum will fill
But what benefit from all this to man shall be?
A new configuration of his bodies shall be seen

Before the bodies of man numbered seven[23]
Representing the seven levels of life in the heavens
But now including the physical, his bodies are nine
Nine levels of life in the cosmos you'll find

Prediction Five

Why do you think it has been
That so little influence from higher realms has been seen
That so little assistance has come to man
That many want to help but so few can?

23. See the Seven Bodies in *Journey to the Heart of God*.

The Stages of Expansion and Contraction in the Cosmos Described by Isis in Prediction Four

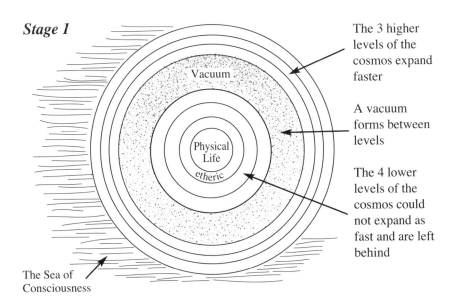

Stage 1

Vacuum

Physical Life

etheric

The 3 higher levels of the cosmos expand faster

A vacuum forms between levels

The 4 lower levels of the cosmos could not expand as fast and are left behind

The Sea of Consciousness

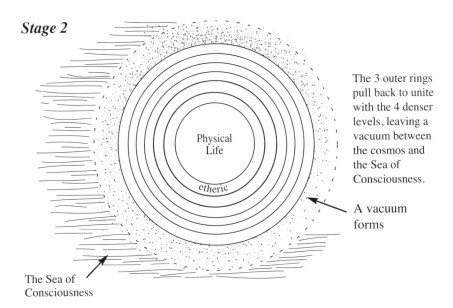

Stage 2

Physical Life

etheric

The 3 outer rings pull back to unite with the 4 denser levels, leaving a vacuum between the cosmos and the Sea of Consciousness.

A vacuum forms

The Sea of Consciousness

(Figure 6)

37

Continued: The Stages of Expansion and Contraction in the Cosmos Described by Isis in Prediction Four

Stage 3

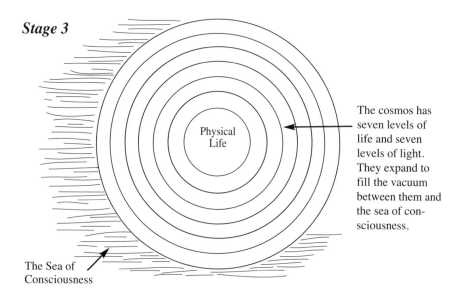

The cosmos has seven levels of life and seven levels of light. They expand to fill the vacuum between them and the sea of consciousness.

The Sea of Consciousness

Stage 4

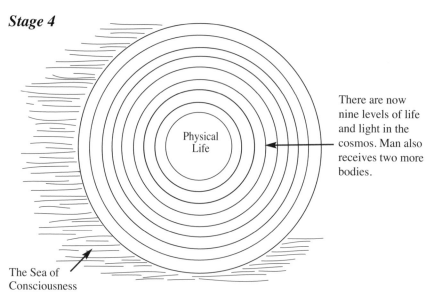

There are now nine levels of life and light in the cosmos. Man also receives two more bodies.

The Sea of Consciousness

This transpired during April-May 2007.

(Figure 7)

The Mother of All, this has done
To save material life from the darkest ones
For their influence too prevented has been
From doing greater damage than what has been seen

Unbeknownst to all a membrane was placed
To safeguard from interference the human race
But humans wondered why none would help
Why they were left to fend for themselves

Many have tried with hearts sincere
To answer the prayers and cries they'd hear
But though they did whatever they could
It did not affect material life as it should

But in the times when the dark ones uncreated will be
An opening in the membrane you'll see
For the first time again assistance will show
First for a few, but then all will know

Mother will open a bit at a time
For those where reason no longer rules minds
Then physical assistance will be seen
No longer only in the etheric realms to be

Prediction Six

First there were seven layers, then there were nine
The layers of the cosmos, will increase in time
But around the cosmos ancient records lay
Now incorporated within the nine are they

Thus beings were formed in the new levels to be
Angels and others not before seen
They embody these records now within
Soon to release them, they will begin

Bodies of magic to aid and assist
To humans will be given, they receive them first
Never before has anyone known
What in this day to man will be shown

As with all magic given, simple it seems,
To hide the wisdom, not by greedy eyes seen
But the pure in heart its import will know
To them alone its secrets be shown

Prediction Seven

The writing I give you will surely change
As more prophecy is given, it will not stay the same
For there's more to the writing than can be seen
The information given is not what it seems

Many layers to understand
Many the changes in your DNA strands
The knowledge I give you light imparts
To carry through blood, wisdom to your heart

Thus the more you read, the more you change
The more within you light can stay
The more light the writing now carries as well
The deeper the secrets my words can tell

The glyphs, more complex will become in time
Changing as read, line upon line
Let your eyes over them freely roam
And the deeper meanings you will be shown

Prediction Eight

When you receive these words of mine
You will have seen how far back in time,[24]
The Mother Goddess attempted to create
The one who would be a perfect mate[25]

But far he was from what She desired
He and his children against Her conspired
The flaw, it would seem, that She did not realize
Was to create him She gave up Her third eye

Why did She do this? Why give part of Herself away?
She hoped to close the gap between them that way
For what She creates could never hope
To be even a fraction of Mother's scope

To make him feel more equal by Her side
This first Mother sincerely tried
As She built him up more and more,
The more he tried to make Her less than before

Why did they both want the differences gone?
Because of what the first Goddess was

---

24. The information was released in *The Gift of the Unicorns*.
25 This refers to the mate, one of Mother's feminine aspects tried to create within the Fall.

41

Like a child She was seeking sameness without[26]
Trying to understand what life was about

She saw only Herself in the mirror of him
But what She saw was Her purity within
So innocent was She when to relate was new
That to conceive children She did not know what to do

Twenty-two levels would life have to fall
Before any offspring were produced at all
He made them like him to form the first tribe
Perhaps he could be equal with them by his side

But tribes will always uniformity seek
That which excels they will try to deplete
For that which is more, shows up their lack
Thus any great being they will try to attack

From child to adolescent, to young adult and beyond -
All these stages throughout the cycles of the Fall can be found
Uniformity changes through levels of diversity
Until at the peak of ascension, within diversity there's unity

But did he innocently live his part in this play?
No, it did not have to be this way
Innocence plundered produces great pain
Trust, once broken, cannot be mended again

Growth can come through adventure and play
A child that is loved learns that way
Instead of learning from what life brought
He sunk into depravity through the power he sought

What highest wisdom within this drama lies?
Although all we've known are the four stages described
And though we thought greatest growth will come
From unity within diversity for everyone

26. For developmental stages within all life, See Appendix VI.

Another stage produces more growth
For before, interdependence depended on those that are low
Now the highest souls will set the pace
The stage of autonomy supports through grace

Explanation: The stage was previously assumed to be the one with the most growth, namely unity within diversity, functioned from interdependence. But with interdependence, the lowest common denominator sets the pace. With autonomy, the most brilliant one accomplishes, and thereby raises all below through grace without effort on their part.

Note: There was indeed a real God of Truth. These first records translated were telling the history of what happened **within** the Fall. We did not encounter the Father, Mother's original first creation, until August 2007 when we left the cycles of the Fall and the imposter gods had been destroyed.

Prediction Nine

There is one prophet revered by most and known to all
Great wonders shall do during the cycles of the Fall
With tricks and magic he shall gain much acclaim
To promote a dark god's masculine reign

At first when he to Earth does come
With others, from Sirius's blue sun
He good will do but then will turn
For his heart too for power does yearn

Disillusionment he brought—many trusted his word
He spoke great wisdom and many heard

Truth can be felt in the hearts of men
He gave just enough truth to mislead them

But he shall not see the reign of peace
For like the others his life will cease
That which he prophesied shall come to be
But its fulfillment he won't be there to see

Prediction Ten

The sacred objects by the Order held
Were given to the Rose to guard them well
Why is it that Thoth these objects did seek
Before his own darkness cause his decease?

They undo illusion because each one of these
Were held by the Mother, for they were keys
To the dark gods' undoing and goddesses too
She blessed them that they would reveal the truth

To the Order She did not reveal what it was they did keep
She knew the dark ones would search their minds when asleep
For the magic to activate within these things
The members of the Order each a symbol did bring

Mother placed these symbols within their hearts
When they met together, the magic did start
The Order held, unbeknownst to them,
The keys to ending the suppression of men

Prediction Eleven

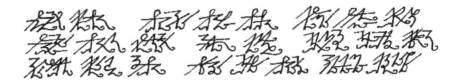

The god Kumara, once among men
Comes to Earth for a short while again
But then he leaves, a most radiant one
To become the god of our planet's sun

The lord Buddha remains faithful throughout
Never assailed by a single doubt
He grows in glory and a planet he rules
The giant Egsplauvitpata stays steadfast too

The goddess of the moon, Elizabeth[27] is called
Gentle of heart and pure of thought
To Mother she an advisor shall be
Where help is needed she shall oversee

An angel assigned, for the Order to send
To anyone whom he needs to defend
Another there is for the Order to ask
For help in healing or any comforting task

One more angel, man's spirit to lift
Is assigned to the Order as a sacred gift
Call upon them, use their sigils and names
They'll help you too if the Order's name you say

These angels' names shall never change
They're written in The Book of Life to stay
The Order of the White Rose magic imparts
That when angels are called, realms come together that have been apart[28]

27. Mother of John the Baptist.
28. When you call the angels' names and sign their sigils, also calling on the assistance of this sacred
    Order, it helps to bring the materialization of Mother's palace closer.

The Angels Assigned to the Order of the White Rose

1. **Ikru-uhurnavetbelichvaheresta:** The one who spreads healing
   wings of comfort

Sigil for Name

Sigil for Meaning

2. **Belevivastlavet-sekrehusba-elechvi:** The one who shields against the
   folly of others

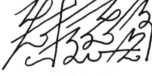

Sigil for Name

Sigil for Meaning

3. **Kruanesta-ulu-egvavistrava-kalaveshpi:** The one who uplifts hearts
   and spirits

Sigil for Name

Sigil for Meaning

(Figure 8)

Prediction Twelve

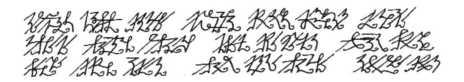

Mother tried but could not understand
That more assistance from Her feminine was not at hand
Why as She suffered, did they not give aid?
Why to Her plight was so little attention paid?

The ones of darkness assistance got
Their higher aspects helped implement their plots
Anyone who tried to help Her was stopped
Thus no assistance was what She got

Throughout the Fall abandoned She's been
The truth by Her at last will be seen
In frustration at the lack of assistance given
During the cycles She full responsibility took for ascension

Her feminine aspects, not Her equal for sure
These aspects diluted and damaged were
When embodied aspects become one,
When all darkness is defeated and done

The physical embodiment of Mother will be
In full interdependence[29] with the Infinite sea
No longer will She carry all alone
She'll do half, Her unformed consciousness some

Then autonomy must be birthed
Not just for Mother, but also the Earth
There is separation consciousness in interdependency
When all is within autonomy there is no identity

29. See Appendix VII.

Explanation: For multiple reasons, described in *The Gift of the Unicorns*, Mother separated out Her feminine aspects so spaces could be created in which the Fall could function. These aspects did not support Her. One of the main obstacles was that they were over-polarized into the place of beingness, rather than doingness. Over-polarization into the feminine created too much passivity.

Prediction Thirteen

Physical gods in those days shall be
But because it came easily, they didn't see
How vast the difference between them and the rest,
Of those still by identity beset

Mother accelerated their development for them
A gift of grace She bestowed upon them
It was necessary for the Earth the archetype to be,
It had to represent all kingdoms of beings

Their identities lost, they only know this
They're as vast as all the cosmos is
No longer trapped in the world of form
At one with all, as though reborn

But the stages of man of which there are three
Mirror that which in the God Kingdom must be[30]
Thus now they are gods and a new kingdom has come,
Old identities gone, there suddenly is a new one

Before with the body identified did they
Then they realized they filled all space

30. See Appendix VII.

But that too is a cosmic identity of a kind
That also in a new way entraps the mind

Thus in the first stage of godhood do they
Find that, though vast they have identity again
Beyond even the far flung cosmic confines
The mind must go to leave identity behind

Mother too must learn the same
For if She doesn't She'll be lonely again
The cosmos really Her light bodies are
But that identity She must go beyond

Let the confines of mind melt away
No longer imprisoned by identity stay
Don't be afraid of the vastness you are
Infinite presence exists wherever you are

Prediction Fourteen

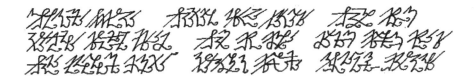

A time will come when Mother will know
That what She's been told is not really so
The six gods and goddesses that to darkness did turn
Were never conceived or created by Her

Part of Her mate's* creation of form,
Without emotional bodies were they born
Through male creation self-centeredness comes
And a fall of consciousness for everyone

But how did the six the ascension survive,
When only those who could feel would stay alive?

* The imposter god created within the Fall–not the real father.

49

Mother's own actions caused this to be
She gave feeling bodies to all generously

But of all his creations, imperfectly made
Not one of them to the Mother true did stay
Their opposite light[31] through ages gone by
Made them reject Mother's great light

Prediction Fifteen

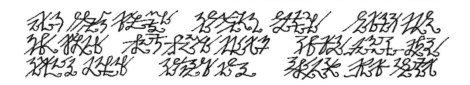

Many have asked in wonderment
Why Mother's love for Earth has been constant
No matter how marred or damaged she's been
Mother's love for her was always supreme

Thus now I'll tell why this is so
It started in the beginning long ago
When Father[32] first formed, they were alone
So She made the Earth to have a home

Long they dwelled with Earth as friend
No other being, just the three of them
The Earth loved Mother and as She fell
The Earth's positive[33] aspects fell as well

Mother created her with a loving heart
Promising her they'd never part
Earth's heart was made full of love to be
The cradle of civilization was she

---

31. This changed in August 2006.
32. The true Father who preceded the Fall.
33. Her masculine, positively charged pole.

No matter how damaged, Mother knew the truth
She remembered Earth's glory during her time of youth
She knew of a time when Earth sacrificed
To be with the Mother she truly loved

Within the Fall, of the imposter god we tell,
Her mate wanted to create as well
At first She told him it couldn't be
He insisted that if She created, why not he

Because She had elevated him right from the start
She over time forgot they were far apart
She finally agreed to let it be so
She wanted to please him though Her heart said "No"

Male creation of matter causes a fall
In creating he didn't use his heart at all
When creations thus formed, imperfect they were
No feeling bodies had they, this was a shock to Her

"Another chance I need to do it right
This time I'll use both love and light"
He continued to plead until She relented
He seemed so sincere, perhaps he'd repented

So Mother allowed it two more times
She wanted to award him for how hard he tried

But he had noticed that weaker She grew
With each fall he was stronger too
So no longer did he permission seek
His imperfect creations, he decided to keep

How Mother Gave Feeling Bodies to All
Excerpt from *Secrets of the Hidden Realms* (2005)

Around the bodies of beings like us that can feel, there are the following fields, the different geometric shapes of which get progressively larger:

A. **Three star-tetrahedrons** (three-dimensional Stars of David). One is stationary, one spins clockwise and one counterclockwise. They all occupy the same space.

B. **Three octahedrons** (two four-sided pyramids base-to-base). Just like before, these three occupy the same space with one stationary and two spinning in opposite directions at a specific ratio.

C. **Three dodecahedrons** (twelve pentagons in the shape of a soccer ball). Just like before, they occupy the same space, one stationary, one spinning left and one spinning right.

D. **Three Flower of Life spheres** *(Fig. 9, How Beings Receive the Ability to Feel)*. Each of the shapes previously mentioned occupy larger and larger areas around the body. Those beings, like the dragons who **chose** not to feel, had **two** stationary fields and one counterclockwise spinning field. Their fields that should have spun clockwise were stationary. In the case of beings who **could not** feel, the Flower of Life spheres had a deformity in the spheres themselves in that—as seen from the front, the right-hand portion of the spheres were incomplete in each of the three fields.

To give them the ability to feel, the following steps were taken:

A. The Flower of Life spheres had to be completed.

B. In all cases, the clockwise and counterclockwise spinning fields had to spin at the proper ratios. This was done by the Angel of the Merkaba, Arahib.

C. They had to be given the necessary endocrine system to produce hormones. This was done by the goddess Panatura.

D. They had to be given the appropriate hormones. This was done by the angel Schatlba.

E. The archangel Metatron then had to use the dispersal energy of the violet flame to remove all old patterns that no longer served.

F. The Great White One, Ascended Master of the Whales, had to sing in the frequencies of the emotions present in a balanced life.

At the time in 2005 when the races of the cosmos were given the edict by the Mother Goddess, "Use your feeling bodies or perish." there were only 600 of Lucifer's great hosts left. Many had ceased to be, as the cosmos was pulled through previous ascension levels. Some had made it

How Beings Receive the Ability to Feel

Beings with feeling bodies have 3 perfect Flower of Life spheres around their bodies. Beings without feeling bodies have 3 incomplete ones.

Steps in becoming able to feel:

1. There need to be 19 perfectly interwoven circles in each Flower of Life Sphere
2. All fields associated with the emotional and mental bodies should be spinning in the right direction and in the appropriate ratio and speeds
3. The necessary glands need to be provided to produce hormones that are needed for emotion
4. Hormones need to be provided
5. Old patterning needs to be removed
6. Frequency needs to be provided that produces balanced emotions

Perfect Flower of Life Sphere

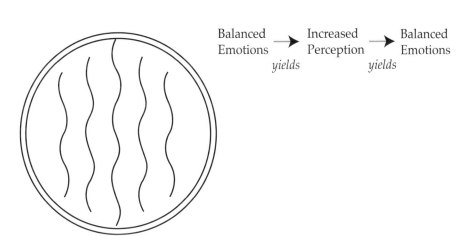

Balanced Emotions → Increased Perception → Balanced Emotions
yields *yields*

Incomplete Flower of Life Sphere

(Figure 9)

into various underworlds, a major evolutionary leap. All remaining had to receive feeling bodies for the further journey of ascension. The entire process took days to accomplish and we could not go through the next gate of ascension before its completion.

Prediction Sixteen

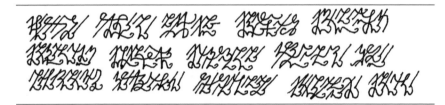

In the Book of Life the Goddess writes
The wisdom of ages, of wrong and right
The law of light it has become
Determining the way for everyone

But hard it was for physical density
To feel the effects of the Book's purity
It's not that its influence was not here felt
But rather that it was too slow to tell

The clock will be brought and then the device[34]
To align and to heal differences in time
And thus its impact more immediately
Is felt within physicality

But what of above? Of the higher realms?
How can the laws of the Book reach them?
Mother will try to send them the Book
But it will come back, though long it took

The answer lies in the lost kingdoms' return
The frequency bands they will bring with them
Shall be laid in the oceans of consciousness between realms

---

34. From the Zhong-galabruk. See The Forgotten Kingdoms later in this book.

That sound can travel beyond, through them

Then the Book must be read, not just written as before
The tones of Mother's voice shall law and order restore
Codes of love in Her dulcet tones
Embracing Her children, calling them home

But now another problem will be found
In higher realms She must slow the sound
Or like the squeaking of mice the sound will seem
And none will know just what She means

Thus the Book in Mother's voice read
Must slow itself to an appropriate speed
Earthly gods and goddesses this secret will discover
They in return will remind the Mother

NOTE: One of the masters on Earth, the Master Ruth, received the following message from the Glaneshveeva (also from the Forgotten Kingdoms).

"Many are seeking, many will find
First you must open the little gold mine
Speak up your truth don't you be shy
We are the round ones you see near by[35]

The Book is written in symbols of love
Speak up and deliver to regions above"

Explanation: They are saying that many are looking for the laws of life and many will find them after the Book is made accessible to them (the little gold mine is opened up). Throughout the ages many have hesitated to advise Mother about that which She may be missing, but it is in being Her hands and eyes and distinct facets of mind that we give the highest service. To be a pristine and pure expression of Her is to fulfill our destiny and we shouldn't be shy about it.

---

35. See the Glaneshveeva later in this book.

They then identify themselves as the beings in the round balls of light the masters present could see. The Mother's language in which the book is written is comprised of 'symbols of love'.

They are telling us it has to be read to higher regions in order to get its message through the vast oceans of consciousness that lie in layers and act as membranes between realms.

Before the restoration of the nine frequencies by the lost kingdoms, and Mother laying them as vast frequency bands into these oceans, sound could now travel through them. This could happen even if the Book could not physically travel through them to be read.

"The Book must be written, the Book must be read
Wrap her in hues of crimson and red
Wrap her in glory, wrap her in praise
Wrap her in sovereign rights of the few
Who dared to be bold, who dared to be true"

Explanation: To protect the book, Mother had surrounded it first in a thick layer of Her light (the glory) and then in a layer of Her blood (red), that no tampering or harm could befall the Book.

Prediction Seventeen

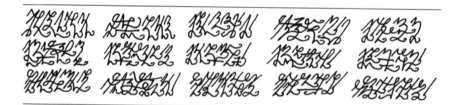

From the stars[36] a language will come
Changing codes of life for everyone
Change shall be for the evolution of all
The codes are kept by those who are small

Hidden they've been inside the sun

---

36. Refers to the little beings from the stars, the Glaneshveeva.

To keep the codes for when the day comes
That the four lower bodies in alignment are brought
That the higher bodies and lower can talk

Unobstructed can information flow
From higher realms to the ones below
Cat magic[37] shall create a wheel most rare
The languages of many shall be there

The wheel shall align not only the bodies of man
Aligning the physical with higher realms, it can
The wheel shall contain many more wheels that spin
In the opposite direction than that of the rim

In the middle a cube stationary will be
On it the language of the Nitzkabelavek you'll see
Great is the day when this wheel turns
The dawning of light among men then returns

Explanation: This prediction tells of a time when the Zhong-galabruk (One of the Forgotten Kingdoms) would bring the design of the alignment device that would align and bridge the gap between the four lower and the five higher bodies of the now nine bodies of man (the microcosm) as well as the cosmos (the macrocosm). The device is called the Estangleuvafli.

---

37. From the Zhong-galabruk the Estangleuvafli shall be brought. This refers to the Forgotten Kingdoms later in the book and the Alignment Wheel, or the Estangleuvafli.

The Alignment Wheel—the Estangleuvafli from the Zhong-galabruk

The middle stationary square is a cube, containing a spinning set of four wheels.
The crystals are the language of the Glaneshveeva.
The crystals are the ninety-six DNA codes of the root races of our enlarged cosmos.
The snake eating its tail means this device also assimilates the past into the present.
The language around the snake (from the Ellamakusanek) speak of spirals of light (their mathematical sequences are: 2, 744, 747, 447, 50/21) placed in the blood to convey information.
Called the Estangleuvafli by the Zhong-galabruk, it aligns the regions, or bodies of the cosmos.

(Figure 10)

One of the Wheels of the Estangleuvafli from the Zhong-galabruk

The Languages are as follows:
The outer ring: Mother's language
2nd from the Outside: The Ellamakusanek (also the three spokes)
3rd from the outside: The Stiblhaspava
The spaces between the petals: The Zhong-galabruk
The large petals: The Bekbavarabishpi
The small petals: The Braamin-hut

(These Kingdoms are described in Book Four)

Trust + Peace + Joy = Adoration
(The meaning of the three spokes)

(Figure 11)

Understanding the Extangleuvafli
The Cube inside the Estangleuvafli

The cube around the center of the wheel that aligns cosmic realms. **A, C** and **D** are written in the language of the Ellamakusanek—they transmitted their images in steams of colour. **E** and **F** have symbols on them from the Nitzkabelavek. **E** is written in the language of the Braamin-hut. They hold the frequencies of the seventh direction once released by Mother (She kept these within her in safe keeping until 2007). *(The sides A, B, C & D were received by the Master Barbara R., The sides E & F were received by the Master Barbara S.)*

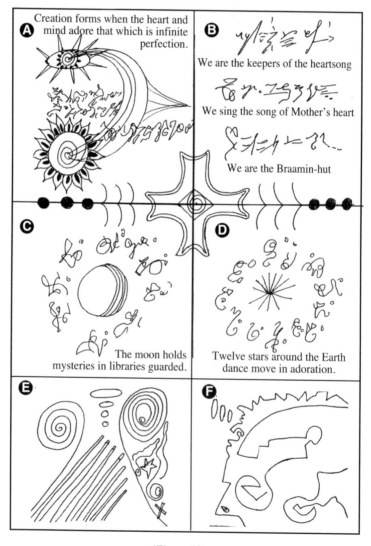

(Figure 12)

The Alignment of Massive Cosmic Clusters

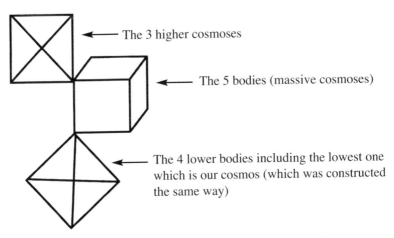

The 3 higher cosmoses

The 5 bodies (massive cosmoses)

The 4 lower bodies including the lowest one which is our cosmos (which was constructed the same way)

The alignment was tilted and twisted. This pattern continues like a vast DNA strand. In April, 2007, Mother created a reverse spin of all beings' DNA. The same is occurring in the macro-macrocosm.

The New Alignment after the device was used throughout the cosmoses.

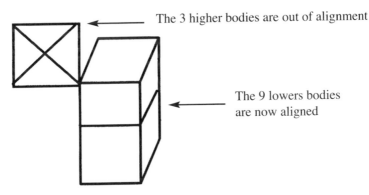

The 3 higher bodies are out of alignment

The 9 lowers bodies are now aligned

Around and in between the cubes lie vast oceans of consciousness, like membranes.

The twelve bodies consisting of massive cosmic cycles were twisted this way.

(Figure 13)

The Center Construction of the Estangleuvafli

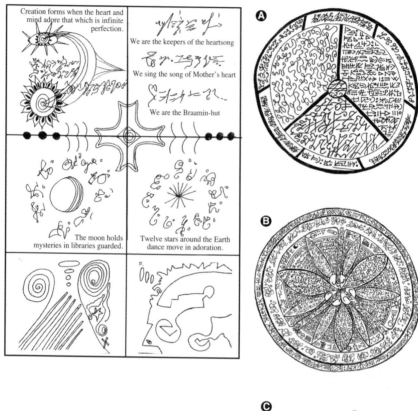

Creation forms when the heart and mind adore that which is infinite perfection.

We are the keepers of the heartsong

We sing the song of Mother's heart

We are the Braamin-hut

The moon holds mysteries in libraries guarded.

Twelve stars around the Earth dance move in adoration.

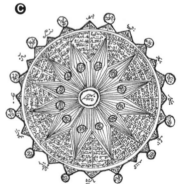

Three of the wheels that intersect each other (the others cannot be given) and spin as a unit inside the cube (its six sides are shown to the left). **A** and **B** do a butterfly wing pulsing motion while rotating with all other wheels.

(Figure 14)

Prediction Eighteen

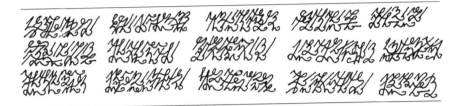

A dragon there is, unassailable is she
Known as Beautiful One, she will come to be
They will try and tamper with her mind
At a time when she'll be the last of her kind

Lonely she'll be, without a friend
But Mother loves her and her mind She will mend
Other dragons[38] there are, but not like her
Of all the dragons Mother shall make her ruler

Once she had a mate, named Dragon was he[39]
She thought he was lost in the consciousness sea
But he was on a mission for the Mother of All
To again come forth when one day She would call

In the center of the Earth's sun was he
Guarding the sleeping ones as was his duty
The little beings that live in stars[40] here were safe
Mother had them hide here in a bubble of space

But time shall be when they shall be free[41]
Then Dragon once again to his love shall flee
Great the joy, she thought she was alone
All of a sudden, her husband has come home

Now another tale of love we tell

---

38. These dragons remained at the top of the large cycles of the Fall. (See *The Gift of the Unicorns*.)
39. See p. 162, *Secrets of the Hidden Realms*.
40. These are the beings known as the Glaneshveeva.
41. They again inhabit the stars around the planet as of May 2007. See *The Gift of the Unicorns* for a description of what 'stars' are.

Of a physical goddess who loved a dragon as well
When her race[42] no longer seemed to be
The goddess to the Mother will appeal

Then a female named Mira Baum Tre Va Se Hay
And a husband with whom she can stay
Will once again by Mother resurrected be
In this way the physical goddess to please

Explanation: The smaller (3'—5' in length) dragon race we encountered during the Earth's ascension, disappeared entirely as we entered higher realms. An earthly goddess requested that Mother restore one that had befriended her. Thus, as a race, they again inhabit Earth. *(Figs. 15, 16, 17)*

Prediction Nineteen

Earth as the cradle of life was scorned
None understood that from her other life was born
Arrogant the gods of Kolob and Melaganiga did become
Thinking that Earth from them had sprung

Vast as planets they surely were
And in the beginning their light was pure
But Mother could see that one day they would forget too
That over all life the Infinite Mother rules

Thus a seed was planted on Earth to grow
Two sacred orders with power bestowed
The one of the Rose and the one of the Dove

---

42. They are a smaller dragon race. See the following depictions.

Depictions of the Smaller Dragons

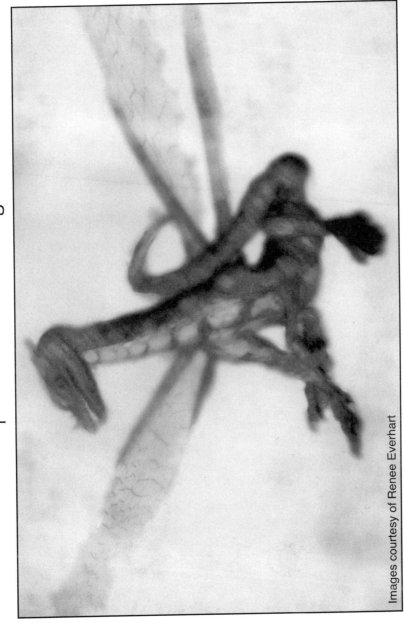

Images courtesy of Renee Everhart

(Figure 15)

(Figure 16)

(Figure 17)

To keep secret lineages of light and love

Authority passed until it was hidden
When with dark ages of illusion man was smitten
Until once more when the Goddess reigns
Then both orders shall be resurrected again

The Gift of Isis

Those who one day these words will read
Will be the ones worthy these words to see
Through the Order prepared from long ago
When the time is right this gift will be bestowed

The sigils[43] I give you, frequency maps are they
To access much power, when illusion is done away
For you to use, joy to restore;
To banish all darkness that went before

Hear now my children your birthright it is
To live a life of abundance and bliss
Be not afraid that you'll go astray
They can only do good, it can be no other way

For the power source drawn from is the Mother Herself
Call with these sigils if you need any help
Great is this gift, the greatest yet given
In the Book of Life these sigils are written

(See Fig. 20 on page 76, The Power Source, Gift of Isis)

Urim and Thummin

The Urim and Thummin were delivered to Joseph Smith, Founder of the Mormon religion and its first Prophet, to enable him to translate the information on the gold tablets revealed to him by the angel Moroni.

43. To understand the difference between sigils and symbols, see *The Gift of the Unicorns*.

There are several references to the Urim and Thummim used by priests of Israel and prophets in the first five books of the Bible and also in Mormon scriptures. They were used by Abraham to view the planet Kolob. Also called seer's stones, the priests from the tribe of Levi wore them in breastplates.

Mormon Doctrine and Covenants: 10:1

"Now behold I say unto you, that because you delivered up those writings which you had power given unto you to translate by the means of the Urim and Thummin, into the hands of a wicked man, you have lost them ..."

Some of these seer's stone devices are still secreted in various sacred sites of the Earth. Among those sites are the hall of records in Ayers Rock, Australia; the hill of Palmyra near Manchester in Ontario County, New York and there are some in Peru, among others.

The Book of Abraham from the Pearl of Great Price[44]

Chapter 3: 1-4 *(See Fig. 18, A Facsimile from the Book of Abraham)*

1. *"And I, Abraham, had the Urim and Thummin[45], which the Lord my God had given unto me, in Ur of the Chaldees."*

2. *"And I saw the stars, that they were very great, and that one of them was nearest unto the throne of God; and there were many great ones that were near unto it."*

3. *"And the Lord said unto me: These are the governing ones; and the name of the great one is Kolob, because it is near unto me, for I am the Lord thy God: I have set this one to govern all those which belong to the same order as that upon which thou standest."*

4. *"And the Lord said unto me, by the Urim and Thummim, that Kolob was after the manner of the Lord, according to its times and seasons in the revolutions thereof; that one revolution was a day unto the Lord, after his manner of reckoning, it being one thousand years[46] according to the time appointed unto that whereon thou standest ..."*

---

44. The Peart of Great Price was translated from Egyptian scrolls by Joseph Smith.
45. See Genesis 12:10 and 20-12 in the Bible; also Exodus 28:30.
46. This was the case before the Earth's ascension began in February 2005.

A Facsimile from the Book of Abraham

Translated Using the Urim and Thummin by the Mormon prophet Joseph Smith

The Mother Goddess bestows authority to rule upon the planetary God of Oliblish (Melaganiga)

The Egyptian Hieroglyphics tell the tale of the Earth's origins in the star-system of Kolob and Melaganiga (or Oliblish). It shows the passing of authority from Mother to Melaganiga. This is the beginning of the sacred orders.

(Figure 18)

the entire ring

These three figures represent the three additional directions, the 5th, 6th and 7th directions that form the horizontal feminine axis of creation. Joseph Smith only mentions the four directions as the 'four quarters', the vertical masculine axis.

Energy pulsed between Oblish as the feminine pole and Kolob as the masculine pole.

(Figure 19)

The Egyptian Papyrus

Translated by the Mormon Prophet, Joseph Smith
With additional translations by Almine

<u>*(See Fig. 19, Unlocking the Mysteries of the Hieroglyphics)*</u>

Explanation

The prophet Joseph Smith purchased an Egyptian papyrus scroll, which is partially shown in Fig. 20. The portions he was permitted to translate tell of the star system of Kolob where the Earth originated.

At the time, he was not permitted to translate portions of the heiroglyphics shown. Almine was permitted to translate five more portions in her book *The Gift of the Unicorns*, but was told the rest is for a later time. In this book she has been given permission to make more translations available. Figures 1-7 are direct quotes from the Mormon scripture, *The Pearl of Great Price*.

Fig. 1—Kolob, signifying the first creation, nearest to the celestial, or the residence of God. First in government, the last pertaining to the measurement of time... One day in Kolob is equal to a thousand years according to the measurement of this Earth[47], which is called by the Egyptians Jah-oh-eh.

Fig. 2—Stands Next to Kolob, called by the Egyptians Oliblish, which is the next grand governing creation ..., holding the key of power also pertaining to other planets...

Fig. 3—Is made to represent God[48], sitting upon His throne, clothed with power and authority; with a crown of eternal light upon his head ...

Fig. 4—Answers to the Hebrew word 'Raukeeyang', signifying expanse, or the firmament of the heavens; also a numerical figure, in Egyptian signifying one thousand; answering to the measuring of time of Oliblish, which is equal with Kolob in its revolution and in its measuring of time.

47. In celestial languages, Melagalinga.
48. Almine's comment; the god of those planets.

72

Fig. 5—Is called in Egyptian Enish-go-on-dosh; this is one of the governing planets also, and is said by the Egyptians to be the Sun and to borrow its light from Kolob through the medium of Kae-e-vanrash, which is the grand Key, or, in other words, the governing power, which governs fifteen other fixed planets or stars, as also Floeese or the Moon, the Earth and the Sun in their annual revolutions. This planet receives its power through the medium of Kli-flos-is-es, or Hah-ko-kau-beam, the stars represented by numbers 22 and 23, receiving light from the revolutions of Kolob.

Fig. 6—Represents this Earth in its four quarters.

Fig. 7—Represents God sitting upon his throne.

Figs. 8—21 (Joseph Smith said that he was not supposed to reveal the meanings of these at that time.)

Information given to Almine regarding figures not translated by Joseph Smith:

Figs. 8—11 May not be translated at this time.

Fig. 12 —The ancient orders or priesthoods will be forgotten then restored.

Fig. 13 —The lower order has a masculine or a more proactive polarity.

Fig. 14 —The higher order is feminine, or receptive in its polarity.

Fig. 15 —Two sacred orders or priesthoods came to Earth from there.

Fig. 16 —The Earth was repelled out of that star-system (of Kolob) and travelled through many star-systems.

Fig. 17 —The Earth had its origins in Kolob. Her name when in this star system was Ana-vi-ash-varuba.

Fig. 18—In the outer ring it clearly states that there is a higher power than the god on the throne, from which all life sprang, and that the higher power is feminine.

Fig. 19—The Mother Goddess created man in Her own likeness.

Fig. 20—The Divine Mother is all-loving and benevolent to all life.

Fig. 21—The Mother's glory is everywhere.

Fig. 22—The god of Kolob is asked to preserve the feminine order of the Mother.

Fig. 23—The god preserves the masculine order of the True Father.

BOOK THREE

The Languages of Mother

The Power Source-Gift of Isis

This sacred diagram of sigils calls upon the Mother's power. The three languages are ones Mother has used during different creational cycles.

(Figure 20)

Introduction to the Languages

Whatever is spoken in Mother's languages becomes reality. Having this power, Her languages and their use constitute a most holy body of white and beneficial magic.

The purity of the languages makes them incapable of being misused. The use of these languages brings light and restores perfection. They are without doubt the most holy symbols on earth.

The languages have provided a guidance system for the cosmos. The choice of a specific language of Mother used during a given cycle of Creation, provided the exact frequencies and amount of light needed at the time.

The fourth language of the Mother has never been spoken in our vast strand of cosmic clusters, but could only be accessed when we entered a parallel strand or reality where we had never been previously, as will be described later in this section.

The Second Language of the Holy Mother
Used during the Cosmic Ascension
(Excerpted from *The Ring of Truth*)

Pronounciation of Mother's Language

The pronunciation is very much like German, other than that the 'v' (as in very) and 'w' (as in white) are pronounced as in English.

The syllables are pronounced individually when placed next to each other. There are no contracted sounds like 'au' (as in trauma). It would be necessary to say the 'a' and 'u' separately. The only exception to this rule is a double 'aa' at the end of a word. This indicates the 'a' sound (as in spa).

The 'ch' spelling at the beginning of a word is the only time it is pronounced as in 'church'. Everywhere else it is pronounced as in the German 'kirche' or somewhat like the Spanish x as in Mexico.

- 'u' is pronounced as in 'prudence'.
- 'a' is pronounced as in 'garden'.
- 'e' is as in 'pet'.
- 'i' is pronounced as in 'pink'.
- 'o' is pronounced in the way someone with an English accent would say 'of' or 'cross'.
- 'g' is always a hard 'g' like 'great'.
- 'c' is always hard as in 'call'.
- 'q' has a 'qw' sound as in 'queen'.
- 'r' is slightly rolled—'rr'.
- 'y' is pronounced as in 'Yvette', with an 'ee' sound.

There are many words for 'I' or 'is' because of frequency changes. "I am happy" has a much higher frequency than "I am tired", and "I" or "am" would therefore be different in each of these sentences.

Also, when the concept is large, several words are needed. 'Beautiful' will have different words depending on what is described, but in each case the term will have several words since it is a complex concept.

There are no words for 'sad', 'pain', 'angry', 'protective' or 'fear', since those are illusory concepts in this creation of life. There are also no negative words.

'I' and 'we' would be the same word as this is a group consciousness language. Similarly, 'he' and 'they' would use the same word.

Sentences and Phrases:

1. *Aushbava heresh sishisim* (Come here)
2. *Va-aal vi-ish paru-es* (Do it again)
3. *Kre-eshna sa-ul varavaa* (It is beautiful everywhere)

4. *Pranuvaa sanuvesh vilsh-savu bravispa* (We are with you when you think of us)
5. *Aasushava pre-unan aruva bareesh* (We come to open the gate)
Note: 'Come' in this sense is not the same word used for 'come here'.
6. *Oonee varunish heshpiu tra barin* (Everyone is dancing with joy)
7. *Belesh bri anur bra vershpi iulan* (Take away the frown from your face)
8. *Nen hursh avervi tranuk averva?* (When comes the moment of laughing?) Note: there is no word for time.
9. *Nun brash barnut pareshvi* (Please take us with you)
10. *Vursh venestu parneshtu* (Magic is in the moment)
11. *Iuvishpa niutrim sarem* (Great things await)
12. *Ruftravasbi iulem* (Let the fun begin)
13. *Verluash verurlabaa mi urla set viunish* (Be prepared for the fulfillment of your dreams)
14. *Be-ulahesh parve mi-ur ville starva* (Speak to us through these sacred words)
15. *Truaveshviesh aluvispaha maurnanuhe* (Welcome to the fullness of our being)
16. *Telech nusva rura vesbi* (Through love are we connected)
17. *Erluech spauhura vavish menuba* (Find the new song that you sing)
18. *Me-uhu vaubaresh ka-ur-tum* (Our new dance is a joyous one)
19. *Pelech parve uru-uhush vaspa pe-uravesh ple-ura* (Together let us create wonderous moments)
20. *Vala veshpa uvi kle-u vishpi ula usbeuf pra-uva* (You are invited into the loving embrace of our arms)
21. *Perenuesh krava susibreve truach* (In great mercy you are renewed)
22. *Pleshpaa vu skaura versebia nunuhesh* (Allow your shoulders to feel lightness)
23. *Verunachva ulusetvaabi manuresh* (All are in this moment redeemed)
24. *Keleustraha virsabaluf bra uvraha* (You dwell in us and are ours)
25. *Keleshpruanesh te le-usbaru* (Call and we shall hear)

(Figs. 21 and 22, The Alphabet of Mother, Fig. 23, The Language of the Holy Mother)

79

Alphabet of The Holy Mother

1. AUX
2. PAH
3. GHEE
4. KA
5. G as in Gold
6. DJU as in Giraffe
7. B
8. PE as in Peg
9. L
10. TRA

11. I as in Ink
12. N
13. R
14. A as in Far
15. M
16. E as in Leg
17. U as in True
18. V
19. SH
20. K

21. H
22. S
23. O as in Open
24. Y as in Yvette ("ee" sound)
25. QW as in Quail
26. T
27. CH as in Church
28. A as in Back
29. O as in Lock
30. XCH as in Mexico (Spanish pronunciation)

(Figure 21)

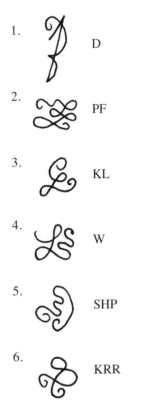

31.   F

32.   Z as in Azure (soft sound)

33.   RR (rolled r)

34.   P

35.   Y as in Yes

36.   CK (short K sound)

37.   Period (placed at the end of a sentence)

38.   Question mark (placed at the beginning of a sentence)

1.   D

2.   PF

3.   KL

4.   W

5.   SHP

6.   KRR

7.   HF

8.  PL

9.   TL

(Figure 22)

The Language of the Holy Mother

Magic is in the
moment. (vursh
venes-tu par-
neshtu)

Great things
await.
(Iuvishpa
niutrim sarem)

Let the fun
begin.
(Ruftra-
vasbi iulem)

Please take me with
you. (Nun brash bar-
nut pareshvi)

(Figure 23)

82

The Body of Magical Incantations for Ireland
From the Mother of All Creation

1. I surrender to the flow of life
Bra u va stichbi satshu u va vesbi kla u taa
Pre u nisbi sta-u-vet blesh pra u vra nesbi sti-u-vaa

2. I am without self-centerdness and ego
Bra u va beshba kla u vestra baa staurat
Kru na ve vaa stiurech vabaa bla-uvatat
Kla u nish pre ru rish uva-trauvat

3. I replace impatience with tolerance
Barsh ba na u va ves plavi
Skaura tra nesh va urespi
Gelshtri satvu menuret
Pil blechvi sta-a-rok preuvet

4. I live a meaningful life through the heart
Tra u bishvaa kre u nit stabaa
Bla u satvi tra-u-bech bilsh vil ste vaa
Gru nit vich versh uris brik belechvi starvaa.

5. I am self-referring for approval
Blaa blas vaa urvechspi balanech staurek steuravet
Vilsh spaa hirsh vaa achvaa stuaret
Mil skla ra vechspi usvaa kletsut manaret

6. I realize my infinite potential
Ske la hishvi klabaresh vi klavanet
Spe u va vechspi bilsh paa varnabet
U-a-lechbi stel hu birsh plavet

7. My being is my sustenance
Paleshu stabalut hechspa urarespi klauvet
Min hursh trauch belchspa vires trua mish baret

8. Each moment I am becoming a greater expression of the perfection of my being

Barich netva arva hursh
Stelaa birsvaa arech nus
Prispraa hesvaa urba setvi baa
Kliu setvaa triu naa
Birtlvit stachvi klesh us bastaa
Hurva nit pre uva silbi hesva-taa

9. I trust in my growing perception and wisdom

Bra bas va vik nichtu birs has vatraa
Pli echvi satru has vra vi us va baa

10. I dedicate my life to the service of the Mother

Ba ruspa hiresh uchvaa arestaa
Tri esh vi A-ru-ma stelavi stechvi ustaa

11. May my work enhance all life

Bresh bras ba taa kri ech vi varustet
Bil eshbi klanuch stelvi birsh bak sta-u-vet

12. My path with heart brings a flow of abundance to me

Birs bra stuvechvi sta u blit bra u-sta-na vik
Sitba eleskru avra vich sta u bla vi setvi nin huravit

13. My home reflects the beauty, love and grace of Mother

Sta bil pre nu vasbi ura-ech vaa kle vu vraa
Bil-esh sta vi u val vu klavunesh pri I Ma-urva servutaa

14. I reflect Mother by living my highest truth

Pelesh virstaa ursvaa vechspi uvaklut
Pri satvu klish Vraa-Maa urstanivu barut

15. I express the love I feel for myself

Birnik blesvaa tra-ug nesvi hareshveg tra-ubit
Erch na klatvu ursvaa staug nar-na-vit

16. I pull in a compatible romantic partner

Barareshvi traunag eles vich va speleru
Birch nasvi kel u trasvaa birs prak par-navu

Vi veshvi skelug bra ura rak spa ves va-vu

17. I am free to express Mother's will through my life without restrictions
Balish presvaa kriutug nesvaa iuret
Pliu setvi kleshbaa Ma-us-vaa kliuvet
Ere vechvi sta-u bilevesbi arch ba vet.

18. I have love and compassion for all beings
Traus biles va kresbi sta-u-vech vaa vi
Kles tru ba arch nun belsh bre sit vu as-vaar-vi

19. I live in eternal time
Barus virna vil pla hes vaa uravach
Birtl birna bil us varas vilsh per vach

20. All illusion of disease is removed from every child
Brachvaa belishvi nanhur varsh
Pilechvaa strachvaa uresvi sars
Kilespaa nus avrevaa hus
Brachnut selvi stravavek blut

21. I live in peace and grace
Balech truas stelvi klasvarut
Selbi kleshvaa urvech stavablut

22. I release all fears
Tre pasvaa kelesvi hech brach bra nas par vi
Granug belech urva birvespi

23. I live with an open heart trusting in the perfection of life
Ba u va spiva alech nusva heresvi
Sti ba us plevataa nuchvi stararok blesbi
Kre u basva sistu-esvi bela bechsbi

24. I replace low self-esteem with visions of my infinite worth
Trach ba ste-u-bi kla-u-vechspi aruret
Mish trechva selvuvaa tra-ba-hesvi-klavunet
Bish nachvaa urech spelvabi sklavuvet

25. I speak fluently
Ste-u-va-vet plesh nit eresvaa
Kli-u ves vaa urva hesva uspataa

26. I sing beautifully
Ste-u-pla us va vet nu stavahu sparut
Nun klesh pri-u-nit selvavu hurarut

27. I create success confidently
Ba uch stavet venush plashet
Ustaa parvi u-berech klanavi
Hersvaa kliu helesbi kresbaa steluch vilesvi

28. I remove the illusion of disease from all
Parsk klaa bra us vaa virich nis veresvaa
Stalich binahur stel u virskla viresvaa

29. I teach a path of light
Tra bish kle u varski birsvaa nihurset
Pre-usvaa keluvrig nan hur avraset

30. My body beautifully reflects perfection
Klaus pirs kla vi argva subatvi hesh
Trech naharvur selbavi klavatur esh
Birsk kla vis peleshvur nanabur barvesh

31. I integrate the material and spiritual realities
Bra skruvanak eleshvi krachvabu stauret
Bel esva bri stararut mish presvi klauret

32. I am able to clearly hear and see the spiritual realms
Kritnut peles vusba vis tele huspa kle-rek nus
Trech urvi stararut pelechvi vara vus

33. I speak my wisdom and truth freely
Ba res pi elech spa uvra vish prech parvi
Nun hesvi klaug spa u rech ru trech varv

34. My life is filled with joy, courage and self-confidence
Tra bich vashvi klesvaa elech nustaver pri parvat

Bru sta vra vi kelush birk nat vilech stra bar vu vas

35. I am free to create my life
Talech vis vatra bi elech nur stavet
Ulech bar usva stela birsk

36. My needs are met effortlessly
Spalech breshva kluaneg
Birspa echva strava hut
Veleshpi skrachva nusvaveg
Rut stanu eles klatvuvet

37. My life is balanced in all ways
Tra va bisva kliunesva kriuta
Bir ha va kresbi struba vesbi varuta

The Third Language of the Mother
Used before the Fall of Creation and restored to Earth March 23, 2007

Introduction

The language illustrated in the following information, given in April 2007 by the Mother, is a language that returned to Earth after the removal of illusion as a reality. All unknown portions of Her Being (illusion) had been solved in August 2006, but the dark gods and goddesses representing illusion lingered until April 2007. When the discordance of their presence in the cosmos was removed, this language in its purity was restored as a gift of enlightenment within the cosmos.

Part I

Ex[49] vi ya sha ush hu vi a su bish va ya
Me u vas ba ux sa ush va us vasta
Yo sa vi pa ux mi hesh pa u neesh
Vel es nus va uf vel e nus ta veesh

---

49. Pronounced like 'Mexico' in Spanish.

You may well wonder where the Fall began
It was long before the descent of man
That the hunger for power created a plan
To subdue the Mother and gain the upper hand

Va ul va vix u va cha u ve
Mi ka ul sa u ba vetch sta u ne
Pelesh pfa uf va bash kya va vish
Mex sta ko e yo ash va nu sa ba va nish

It is with joy that a king of truth[50] is found
When in gods' hearts only greed abounds
But great is the grief to Mother's heart
As She discovers his heart is dark

Ka ush mish kanash ula ve kya u ya
Mish va stua vi a ax nush vya u
Os kyo ush na shu sha shaan
Viya yo sta u nesh vi ash vastaa

Of the gods of the Earth revered by man
But few could the test of power withstand
Most were swept away this day[51]
Condemned by their hearts, they could not stay

Alsh vaa sta u bash va e yo
Pa lux bi ya ka vish vel stash u va so
Mix kya no se va klua uush ma u naa
Pfe elex cha vaa unes staa

Among men, gods and goddesses too
Through ascension raised, to godhood new
Fell from their former high estate
Few there were that kept the faith

Ush kush vas ba vi elsh klaa u na vix
Sta u va yo kna u vish ma na nix

50. He was not the real Father, but an imposter.
51. April 2, 2007

Kelesh u staa pelsh nu kya va u nu
Usha sha naa balex nus us staa vu

This is the day the nine great lords
Who once governed light from Amenti's Halls[52]
Fell from power and ceased to be
Because of their treachery, lust and greed

Ba aalsh nu vie klas va sut va klex va taa
Mix kyaa vaa u ox tchaa nana vyaa
Shpa su shu ash va us kye nu na te
Mitchaa ex kye belesh baa kla va ye

A day of purging of once trusted ones
Preparing for a time of purity to come
When love shall flow forth to everyone
The reign of the Goddess has begun

Part II
Received from the Mother, April 3, 2007

Viya se pa ush ta a va vexh spa u
Va vesh ta ubaxh ya sta va.
Mixh kiyè su uva vish tya ba u va veesh cha unaxh
Pè i ye keu cha u viva uva bya

The way of ascension Earth was to take
By dark ones blocked, was difficult to make
Often she tried, as often she failed
On that route too many entrapments lay

Kye usta u elesh vyi ax vaunesh
Ba u vyi esva ucha vaa
Pyè kya uva viesh sta uva bya ka
U vyesbi uva vish byex kava

Thus Mother stepped in to find a way
That she no longer in density stayed

52. For more information on the Halls of Amenti, see Appendix II.

Wayshower to all she had become
For the cosmos she was the archetypal one

Ka vash kya va uva vesh biyè
Cha u ni va viesh ba u neesh
Kyes pa kyesh cha va ustè
Velesh biyexh usta pa u vanyex

Over the edge of space she did ascend
Pulling the cosmos over the bend
Leaving the dark gods to rethink their plans
To try and stop her if they can

Bau kya u spa ba vi klaesh usba
Klau vex bi sta u kla vaa us
Tya u pfyos ba usta biex klash
U na viesh kla u hesh bi esh

But many of us had lost pieces of ourselves,
Dragons and fairies, giants and elves
All were waiting for us on the route
That was abandoned by us—the one we ascended without

Vyioch kelesh ta u va ni-ex
Skla us ta u viyesh sta u na
Knu us sta u kyès ba kli ex
Kla ush cha-usta pli ex na
Us stex kla u kyes ba ux
Cha na nex ki-u belesh bla-a

But that was not all we left behind
Forgotten kingdoms, three of that kind
Each secrets and information held
Each had magic and mystical spells
Thus were those realms called this day[53]
All that was pure could join us to stay

Balu viyex sta u vish kla-u vaa

53. April 14, 2007

Kya biyex bi u velesh vi klikla ustaa

When darkness was banished great was the cost
But the new life now would make up for the loss[54]

The Language of Mother Spoken in the Ocean of Consciousness

Introduction

It was in the last week of April 2007 that, for the first time I spoke to a vast and unformed aspect of the Mother Goddess: the Mother of the Ocean of Consciousness. I had asked the Darklings (see Book IV, the Forgotten Kingdoms) whether She existed as limitless consciousness, thinking that, as the cosmic history keepers, they would know. They had no information about anything outside our cosmic boundaries, however, and felt sure no one else did either.

I asked the Mother of the Ocean of Consciousness if She had a boundary. Although She spoke very slowly, the silence that followed suggested She had never comtemplated such a question before. She said She had no knowledge of this, but would look into it. For four days I asked whether She had an answer, but She did not. On the fifth day, She said: "There are Others like Me in higher frequencies, separated by membranes."

Part I

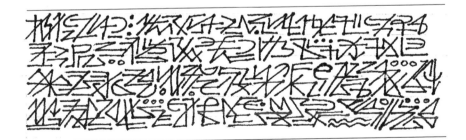

---

54. There had been a loss of diversity and portions of kingdoms when illusion dissolved. However the diverse life forms on the ascension route we did not take, were called into our cosmos and made up for the loss.

Balak uvefri skala hes pet kelavu
Stuba uskala lok hustaba uvrate
Mik gernik ukle vilaves. Pru u staba.
Ri u belespa unavik uste u afla ba.
Kil het lanes sta. U kratl vi u belech
Not u stech va bi kla u beret u nit.
Prek u biritl verkl us sta vaa.
Nen herch ubla uvef fra bi
Us klat net hes pa u vi

I tell you now of that which seems
But an endless consciousness sea
It too divided is, membranes separating between
What you would call a 'vacuum' is there

Before individuation forms again
Membranes above and below, consciousness within them
There oceans separate cycles so vast
In these cycles the future meets past
Like a closed circuit that never ends or starts

The Book of Life Mother tried to send[55]
To cycles above, but it came back again
Thus the laws of life could not reach them
Unknown they lie to infinity's end.

But what is above that has made us descend?
Many times we've been here, only to go down again.
This time ascension has a different end.

55. See Predictions of Isis, 16.

Part II

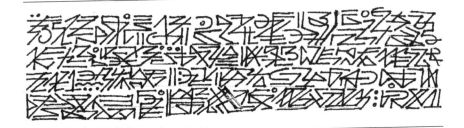

Krua u stakva u heres tra vi
U peles bik helesvi sku at va uva set
Birtl kirsbak nun het vi skuluk
Tranu uska ba. Virit vi ustavekvi
Bel u sat pelesvra. Knus as va
Tra u klabarut uva ples bi skele stut
Pirs has da us pava krit nin hurt kla u ba

Gerek u stak va u tek. Bertl letvi Kelesva.
Tru stak tek hetvi usva ek bret paletvu.

The bands of compassion[56] great frequencies are
Building blocks of life that is or ever was
Each with a quality all of its own
Four there are that you have known

Three there are that no longer exist
Of the original four only one now is
Unity within diversity and autonomy too
Only in material life will you find these two

Nine bodies[57] of light inside the cosmos you'll find
Separated by membranes, in the oceans of consciousness lie
Something different than ever has been
Three more bands of compassion, never before seen

---

56. See *Journey to the Heart of God* and Appendix VI.
57. Man too received nine bodies instead of seven in May 2007.

Their qualities are for you to discover
They are new in the cosmos, placed there by Mother
But the levels of life as a result will raise
Beings will relate in new and different ways

Explanation: As set forth in Appendix VI, prior to May 2007 the bands of compassion forming the building blocks of existence, mirrored the stages of growth found in all life. Those stages were: uniformity, diversity within uniformity, diversity and unity within diversity.

The Mother of the Ocean of Consciousness informed me that during May 2007 the bands of uniformity, diversity within uniformity and that of diversity ceased to exist. The only one of the original four building blocks that still exists is unity within diversity.

She explained that unity within diversity (interdependence) and diversity within unity (autonomy) still exist only within physicality. She said we must discover the other two bands of compassion, since all relationships will change as a result of that knowledge.

Part III

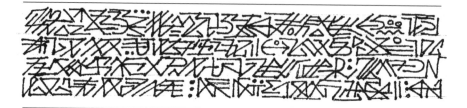

Sta lik vi ubasva klet ut set ba usaba
Geres pavabi erikva klunas tek eshbi granastik uvla avra bit.
Gel sta uplefbi ukrana stik ublavi.
Erekstavi ukla ustava ubra plef

Interdependency not by the need dictates
You may be good at what you hate
What is contributed must be a path with heart
Or otherwise the unity falls apart

Thus if you feel you cannot comply
With what others expect, even after you try
Free are you to state your truth
That they know to replace you

Autonomy, on the other hand
Is a whole new frequency to understand
It doesn't mean all responsibility to shun
But it does mean freedom for everyone

The one with the most responsibility
Also has most freedom to steer his destiny
To seek from others detached to be
Is independence, an obsolete frequency

Autonomy belongs to a sovereign being
Whose sustenance always comes from within

Explanation: In unity within diversity, the unity comes from a common vision, but the vision cannot override the desires of the heart. In autonomy there is diversity within unity. The unity is based upon a common bond of the heart, or love. Love creates the bond, but within that the highest guidance comes from self-responsibility.

Part IV

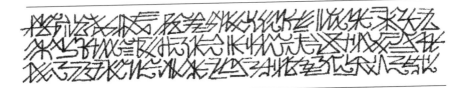

The "God of Truth", as the imposter is known,
Has much pain and destruction sown
Thus first uncreated, then re-created I him
But always he chose on Me to turn

When he was not there and into the ocean dissolved,
Stagnation occurred and had to be solved

When in his evil deeds he was bound
More powerful the higher aspects of him I found

There seemed no end to his tyranny
The higher he was, the more power had he
Everywhere I reached he appeared to be
Setting his lower aspects free

I decided he should not the first creation be
Instead of one, there would be three
Horlet, Sunat Kumara, Egsplauvitpata always faithful had been
Thus as the first born they the template would be

But they would always be under threat
For in regions above he would fume and fret
How could we find rest? How could we find peace?
A permanent threat; how could we be at ease?

I could not reject him for he was part of Me
Thus I would re-absorb him back into Me
He would not dissolve into the consciousness sea
Thus empowerment instead of stagnation there'll be[58]

And so I discovered to My surprise
The restoration of My third eye
Depended upon his merging back into Me
Moments after his creation when he was yet pristine

Every conceivable loop, every circle of life
Wherever the imposter you can find
All must be absorbed in the very same way
Forever inside My physical[59] body to stay

Note: The following eight verses are explained in the latter portion of
Part V.

---

[58] She found stagnation resulting within the cosmos when She tried to dissolve him entirely as a creation. Re-absorbing him back into Her body produced empowerment instead.
59. The denser, positive aspect of Mother.

The three as the male templates are
Forty-four cosmoses times nine it is so
But realms above that are not as below
There for a while he will be, you must know

But sealed I have the above from below
By the power of My blood I have made it so
That in the forty-four times nine, all life may grow
That there at last peace they'll know

How do we keep him from finding a way
To reinstate chaos by a powerful display?
Is there not more power in the heights where he dwells?
Listen My children, a secret I'll tell

We have been at the bottom, but not any more
The cosmos we're in is not as before
Instead of attempting to forge ahead,
The cosmos shall grow the opposite way instead

Then the last shall be first and the first shall be last
And so as we grow we shall assimilate the past
For as a snake that its own tail does eat
We shall gather more strength as the way we'll lead

But tired are the beings in our cosmos of growth
Much of strife and little of peace they've known
They yearn for rest and they want a home
The stress of growth most in the upper realms have shown

To alleviate burdens and ease their pain
I a plan to internalize the growth have made
The light from assimilating him and aspects of Me
Shall enter only Me, but to the cosmos reflected shall be

The growth to the cosmos thus shall be slowed
That finally a time of rest they'll know
This shall hasten the glorious day
When visible to all, on Earth My palace shall stay

Part V

I'll tell you now a secret most true
One day you'll go far beyond what you previously knew
To find that the largest perspective you see
Can be so much more than you thought it could be

Like a large strand of DNA, cosmic clusters lie
But eleven more strands like these around our strand does lie
Parallel existences in which you all live
Communication between these can flow through the wheels that I give

Nine strands of cosmoses, like pearls upon a string
Can through their purity aid to this cosmos bring
Two others corrupted have been, by male gods made so
Do not open the gates to them before it's time to do so

Realms ten, eleven, twelve, parts of the strand this cosmos is in
The strands of cosmoses number five and twelve all have corruption
    within
They know not that cosmic strands like them exist
To have this knowledge, this cosmos is the first

Explanation: These cosmoses represent a reality parallel to ours.
Because man is the microcosm, contemplating the wheels given, activates higher codes within our DNA.

On June 1, 2007, with the assistance of the wheel shown in Fig. 25,
representing the 2nd cosmic cluster's strand, a passageway, or tunnel,
was opened between our cosmic strand and theirs (the parallel strand, or
reality). The objective was to transmit the Book of Life that contains our

The Twelve Strands of Cosmic Clusters

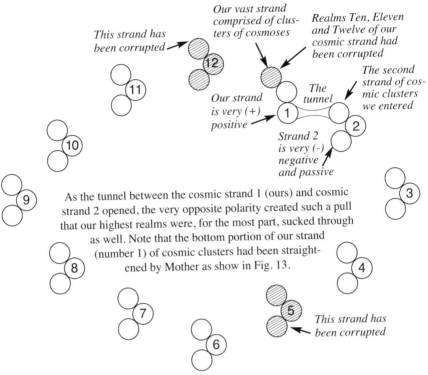

This strand has been corrupted

Our vast strand comprised of clusters of cosmoses

Realms Ten, Eleven and Twelve of our cosmic strand had been corrupted

Our strand is very (+) positive

The tunnel

The second strand of cosmic clusters we entered

Strand 2 is very (-) negative and passive

As the tunnel between the cosmic strand 1 (ours) and cosmic strand 2 opened, the very opposite polarity created such a pull that our highest realms were, for the most part, sucked through as well. Note that the bottom portion of our strand (number 1) of cosmic clusters had been straightened by Mother as show in Fig. 13.

This strand has been corrupted

Vast DNA-type strands of cosmoses lie in clusters of twelve, as shown. Our cosmos is part of one such strand. We had cleared the bottom part through the ascension but the top corrupted part had to be sealed off.

The More Physical Strands:
Strands 1 through 6 have four realities happening simultaneously. A cross section of a cosmic cluster in one of the strands would look like this:

The More Spiritual Strands:
Strands 7 through 12 have twelve realities happening simultaneously. A cross section of a cosmic cluster in one of the strands would look like this:

In all 12 strands of cosmic clusters, a total of 96 realities are found. There are 8 clusters of 12 such strands. A total of 96 strands exist.

(Figure 24)

Wheel Representing the 2nd Cosmic DNA Strand, Consisting of Cosmic Clusters

These cosmoses represent a reality parallel to ours. Because man is the microcosm, contemplating the wheels given, activates higher codes within our DNA. This wheel is called *Estranguvachbilshetnenhurvi*.

(Figure 25)

strand's highest wisdom. *(Fig. 24, The Twelve Strands of Cosmic Clusters)*. Our cosmic cluster's strand represents the 'physical' of the twelve strands. It is in the physical where all new knowledge is gained. Therefore, it is also the place where the most growth occurs and the most wisdom is gained.

Not only did the Book of Life go through, but because our frequency and light is much more positively charged than that of the parallel reality, more than half of our highest realms were also sucked through. This irresistible pull was the result of opposite polarities in light and frequency attracting.[60] Those are the kingdoms representing the ninth body of the cosmos, such as the Darklings, the Ellamakusanek, the Zhong-galabruk and all the other 'lost' kingdoms that had recently returned. Many of them were killed in the congestion.

On June 3, 2007, Mother resurrected those who had perished and called back those who had gone through the tunnel. To those resurrected, it seemed as though they had hardly been gone at all (we had synchronized our clocks[61] with that of our higher realms, so for them only a day had passed as well). For the others who had passed through the tunnel, millions of years had passed since they had left. The much higher frequencies of the other strand had created a far different passage of time.

What seemed like a catastrophe at the time, had a great number of benefits, however:

- The kingdoms of the ninth level of our cosmos had borne the brunt of the unremittant rapid growth of the cosmic expansion and ascension. They were tired. The Darklings had said, "It would be nice to be home—to rest". The blissful, expanded inactivity of the second strand had given them a chance to rest and recuperate. When Mother resurrected those who had perished, they too were rejuvenated.
- They returned with a renewed appreciation for the adventures and even for the hardships of our cosmos. In the parallel cosmos, very little change and growth occurred during the millions of years they were there. For those who had been gone, great joy was felt at being reunited with those they had not seen for what seemed to them, millions of years. These positive emotions boosted our cosmos.

60. See *The Ring of Truth* for information about light and frequency having their opposite poles attract.
61. The clock, used to synchronize everyone's passage of time, is depicted later in the book.

- They had assimilated higher light and frequency and boosted the highest levels of our cosmoses with 10% more light and higher frequency. The ninth body accesses potential and produces awareness. Those who had been pulled through will now aid in producing more potential-laden awareness throughout the cosmos.
- The Darklings had left the history of the cycles of life of our cosmoses with the other strand and have in turn brought their history back for us to learn from. This has helped change their innocence to wisdom; the way one grows by watching a movie, rather than having to actually experience the events shown.
- The Ellamakusanek were able to give them spirals of light within their bloodstreams that enabled communication to take place between their strand and ours.
- The Zhong-galabruk were able to synchronize our time to theirs so they could support us as the point of greatest growth of the All. Our accelerated growth will become theirs. They were also given the frequencies of the 12 pairs of pure emotions as well as the 12 pairs of states of being and the 12 pairs of heart energies. These are more fully described in the Bonus Section, part V.
- The kingdoms jointly gave them the necessary frequencies, just as they did for us, to fill the 'voids', or membranes, between cosmoses so that the Book of Life can be sent from cosmos to cosmos within the second strand through Oceans of Consciousness.
- They have brought from the second strand the languages needed to create similar tunnels to the other 10 cosmic DNA strands.

Note: In the microcosm, our 12 DNA strands represent our 12 bodies (humans are aware of and accessing only nine light bodies as of June 2007). The two visible strands (the others are made of sub-atomic particles) represent our physical and etheric bodies.

The etheric strand holds the linguistic records. When entering the God-kingdoms, as described in *Secrets of the Hidden Realms*, accessing languages from other kingdoms comes easily, since the etheric and mental bodies are merged into one at this stage of man's evolution. The mind can then access these linguistic records. Ancient Taoist writings speak of the immortal masters among them suddenly being able to speak other languages as they enter their mastery.

In the macrocosm, our strand of cosmic clusters represents the physical, and cosmic strand number two represents the etheric realms of the All.

Song of Rejoicing by the Braamin-hut[62] upon their Return
From the Parallel Reality

Es blah pru pranavik bilish ba hur spa ura vit

Praise to the Mother of our universe
Who birthed life forms beautiful and diverse

Kaliknesh pre usbariz beleru pernik helstavaa

For nowhere else can so many flowers be seen,
Nor do the waters with glistening fishes teem

Uru zur ba ukles vi astra nun hu bising

Praise to all lives from which wisdom was borne
Where courage was forged and loyalties strong

This song is by Raiijig
(one of the Braamin-hut)

62. See Book IV.

Wheel Representing the Third Cosmic DNA Strand Consisting of Cosmic Clusters

The Wheel is called *Gereneesh-hasvi-stereruch*.

(Figure 26)

Wheel that Accesses the Past of Our Strand of Cosmic Clusters

This wheel accesses the 10th, 11th & 12th bodies of our cosmos. At one point they had been our future but then we side-stepped them by entering the second strand of cosmic clusters. They then became our past. It is from these higher realms that changed from our future to our past, that the Wingmakers[63] archaeological finds originated.

63. Information is available on www.wingmakers.com.

(Figure 27)

Part VI

I tell you now what you should do
In this message there's caution for you
Incorporate the other strand, as you must
Their primary god at last you can trust

But know My children what you will find
That the nature of this strand corrupts the mind
Each strand looks at life differently
Bring him here and he too corrupted will be

Not only the second, but the fourth and the sixth too
Shall become corrupted, though now they're pure
To go into them, you must find the way
Let them not come to this strand of DNA

Concern not yourself that the three higher realms will be left behind you
Leave behind three levels, but gain forty-eight in strand two *(See Fig. 28)*
That you shall blend into yourself
And from those highest levels your old strand you can help

For in your old strand also forty eight levels you'll find
Except for the lower, corrupted they all are in kind
Strand two the most feminine of all, it is
Bring all strands there; an advantage in this

For its perception by nature is inclusive
And all strands will greatly benefit from this
Combine the ones that uncorrupted are
Then to tackle the others you'll be stronger by far

I give you a wheel to enter from the top;
That the Book you can send and none shall it stop,

Our Strand and Strand Two of the Cosmic Cluster

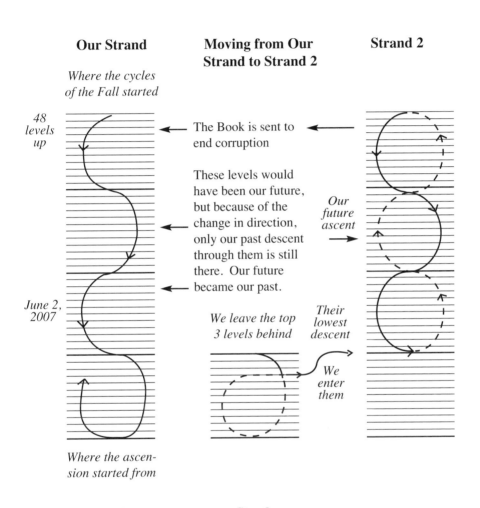

Our Strand

Where the cycles of the Fall started

48 levels up

June 2, 2007

Where the ascension started from

Moving from Our Strand to Strand 2

The Book is sent to end corruption

These levels would have been our future, but because of the change in direction, only our past descent through them is still there. Our future became our past.

We leave the top 3 levels behind

We enter them

Strand 2

Our future ascent

Their lowest descent

Step 1
We ascend back up where we came from. But A, B & C are corrupted.

Step 2
9 levels up we leave our strand and move into strand 2.

Step 3
We enter into the second strand of cosmic clusters where there is no corruption.

(Figure 28)

That an end can come to a terrible reign
And your strand of cosmoses be whole again

Entering the Second Strand of Cosmic Clusters

To have tried to tackle the opposition of A, B and C from where we were in June 2007, would have been futile. Strengthening ourselves by assimilating strand two into our strand would have corrupted them as well. We therefore entered strand two, and after easily ascending to the top, could first send the Book of Life to our original strand, and then pull it into us after dissolving their treacherous gods. *(See Fig. 28 Our Strand and Strand Two of the Cosmic Cluster)* Most feminine of all DNA strands of cosmoses, therefore the most inclusive.

If we were to enter them, the inclusive and more passive traits would dominate and benefit life for our cosmos. If, on the other hand, they entered us, their male god would become corrupted by the nature of our strand, which is separative and prone to corruption.

Mother says we should not concern ourselves with leaving the top, corrupted levels of our strand behind in moving through the tunnel. We would gain more than we would lose. She gives a wheel that can be used to access the higher levels of all twelve DNA strands of cosmoses (the C and D levels. *(See Fig. 32)*

She recommends combining all uncorrupted cosmic strands into strand 2 in order to benefit from its loving and inclusive perspective.

This gateway opens up the A or B levels of all cosmic DNA strands. It also opens the higher levels of C, D and E and F. *(See Fig. 28)*.

Wheel of the Fourth Cosmic Strand of Cosmic Clusters

Contemplating these wheels activates the potential encoded as dormant information within our DNA strands. This gateway to the 4th strand of cosmic clusters
is called *Spa-uvravechspabrihubrahuvravechshpri*.

(Figure 29)

The Wheel of the Sixth Strand of Cosmic Clusters

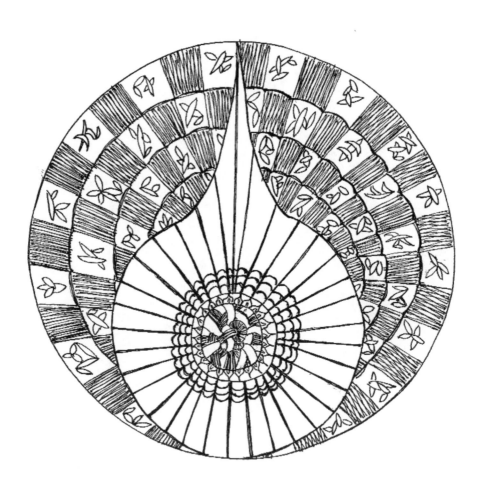

This wheel is called *Klarsvirishespistravavut*.

(Figure 30)

Wheel of the Seventh Strand of Cosmic Clusters

The name of this gateway to the seventh cosmic DNA strand is
Dauvastracharuvishva.

(Figure 31)

Part VII

Great are the changes though subtle at first
When you enter the second strand from the first
New codes from the Mother for man's DNA
Will make him respond to life in different ways

Huge evolutionary leaps for all species there'll be
New species from the new strand in nature you'll see
Ninety six codes given first to humanity
But then other star-races too recipients will be

The physical strand in man's DNA had become dominant
But now the more inclusive qualities of the second strand will be prevalent
Now is the moment of chance to rise above the past
But then you must throw off social conditioning at last

Be careful what you give your attention to
For the future is at this time shaped by you
Carefully selected the readers of these sacred words,
Only by the holy ones will these words be heard

These are the ones who great influence wield
Their every action great results will yield
Let not your entertainment be violent and cruel
Seek out in silence that which is pure

Although you cannot see the journey's end
Be of good courage, great strides have been made
Every kingdom shall henceforth change
Like ripples in a pond, forever it extends

The secrets given by Isis you'll read

Not always in written form has been
The symbols and wheels that have been revealed
Should be contemplated their change to yield

This is a time when subtle information
Can far more effectively yield its revelations
For of all the strands that through eternity lie
The one you've entered is the most feminine by far

The Warning from Mother

Because strand 1 and strand 2 are representative of the two furthest extremes of masculine and feminine polarities, they are also most attracted to one another. The further polarities (there are degrees in polarities) are apart, the bigger the pull between them (this pertains to light and frequencies; with matter and energy opposites repel). For this reason, the Mother issued the following warning:

Although I have given you the wheel, *(See Fig. 32)*
The tool to enter strand one when you wish
Remember My children what happened to you
When the higher kingdoms were sucked into strand two

The pull between the strands is very strong
To open up a gate too soon would be a choice that is wrong
Levels thirteen through twenty-four of that strand most masculine are
Levels thirty-seven through forty-eight are more feminine by far

Wait thus until you can send in the Book to the levels of which I speak
Reducing the gap in polarity and the pull in between
Then take the precautions I soon will tell
Send in the Book and all will be well

A hologram exists in the place you have been
I maintain it, that your departure remains unseen
And until they join you, so it will be kept
None shall know of another strand to where you have left

The Gateway to the Upper Levels of Twelve Cosmic Clusters

This gateway opens up the C or D levels of all cosmic DNA strands.
It also opens the higher levels of B, E A & F.
See Our Strand and Strand Two of the Cosmic Clusters, Fig. 28.

(Figure 32)

The Gift of the Ninety-Six New Codes

The Ninety-Six New DNA Codes Given to Man
For a Jump in His Evolution (June 8th, 2007)

(Figure 33)

(Figure 34)

(Figure 35)

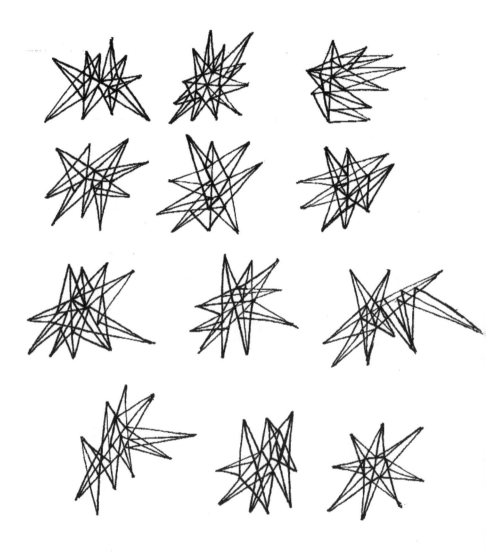

(Figure 36)

118

(Figure 37)

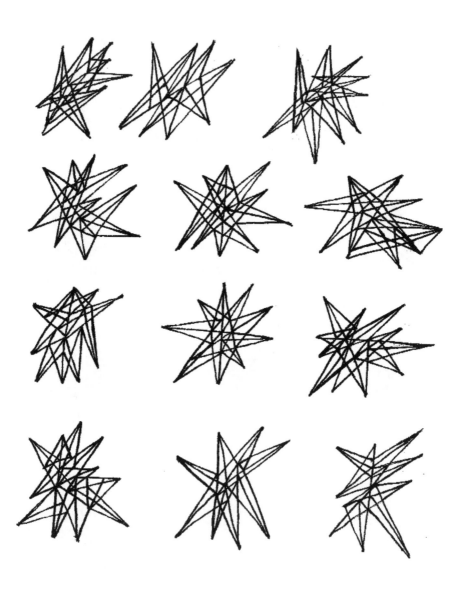

(Figure 38)

(Figure 39)

(Figure 40)

The Gift of the Ninety-Six New Codes

These 96 new DNA codes that are now a gift from the Goddess to all species, replace the 96 that are on the device from the Zhong-galabruk, the Estangleuvafli.

I was in France during the 8th of June, 2007, when I suddenly got the urgent message that I needed to ask the Mother Goddess to place something into the Book of Life. After searching for some time for what could possibly be the problem, I found out that the cosmic DNA was in the process of being changed and soon every wheel, that I had spent hours drawing exactly as I had seen it appear before me, would become obsolete. Thankfully, Mother put in the Book (and whatever She puts in the Book becomes reality), that their meaning would not alter as did the building blocks of reality: the codes of the DNA. This meant they would not loose their function and significant meaning as reality changed.

What the Ninety-Six Codes of Existence Represent

The cosmic DNA is divided into 12 strands as we have seen. Each of these 12 strands forms a cluster and there are 8 such clusters. The twelve strands each have more than one parallel reality (what we call petals). To understand these realities that run simultaneously to ours, think of four stage performances going on at the same time. Each play has the same actors and the same script. Each interprets the script in a different way, thereby maximizing learning opportunities.

Each of the first six DNA strands of each of the eight clusters has a total of four petals or parallel realities going at once. These six deal with the denser realities. The second group of 6 strands, interpreting the higher realities, has 12 parallel existences each. The total number of petals or existences lived in each cosmic strand is therefore 96. Within the 8 clusters of 12 strands each, there is a total of 96 strands. Man as that unique microcosm, reflects these 96 ways of interpreting reality, through his 96 DNA codes in his cluster of 12 DNA strands (only two are visible, as the other 10 consist of sub-atomic particles).

On the small scale, even the most minute of details reflect the large picture. For example: The jump in parallel realities goes from four per strand to 12 per strand—a three-fold jump. In 2005 (see *Secrets of the Hidden Realms*), I was told that there were 32 root races in the cosmos and we were given their DNA codes, now there are 96—again a three-fold jump. There are, as explained, also a total of 96 DNA strands, or strings of cosmoses, in the 8 clusters of 12 strands each within the Infinite's being: the macro-macrocosmos.

The DNA strands are in pairs *(See Fig. 24)* that reflect the exact opposite of each other's polarity. For instance our original strand (strand number one) was the most masculine of all the strands. The number two strand, of all the strands is the most feminine—number one and number two strands are paired. It is for this reason that Mother advised that all other strands be brought into the number two strand, and not the other way around. Being the most feminine, the way reality is accessed within this strand, is the most inclusive and the least able to be corrupted.

Our Original Strand's Four Loops of Existence

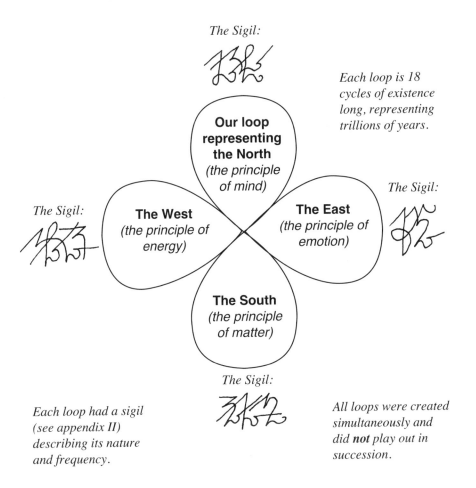

The Sigil:

Our loop representing the North *(the principle of mind)*

Each loop is 18 cycles of existence long, representing trillions of years.

The Sigil:

The West *(the principle of energy)*

The East *(the principle of emotion)*

The Sigil:

The South *(the principle of matter)*

The Sigil:

Each loop had a sigil (see appendix II) describing its nature and frequency.

*All loops were created simultaneously and did **not** play out in succession.*

The Name for All Four Loops is: Kelesh-usva-trabach-heruhit

After successfully completing its ascension cycles, our loop in the north had all other loops join with it into one, in January 2007.

(Figure 41)

The Strands of Cosmic Clusters Within the Infinite's Being

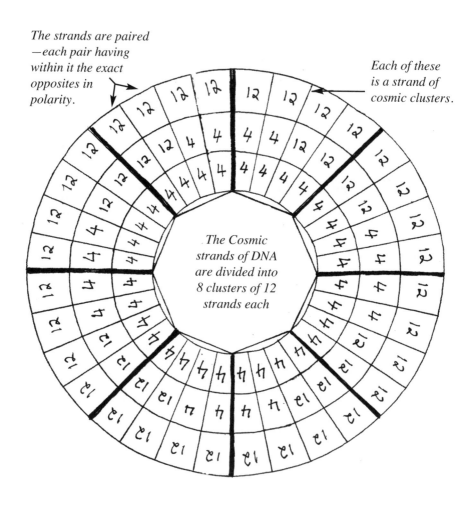

The strands are paired —each pair having within it the exact opposites in polarity.

Each of these is a strand of cosmic clusters.

The Cosmic strands of DNA are divided into 8 clusters of 12 strands each

The numbers indicate how many parallel realities each strand has. Every strand with 4 petals, or parallel realities, has 48 levels within it. Each strand with 12 realities has 96 levels within it.

(Figure 42)

The Codes of the Ninety-Six Strands of Cosmoses Found Within the Infinite

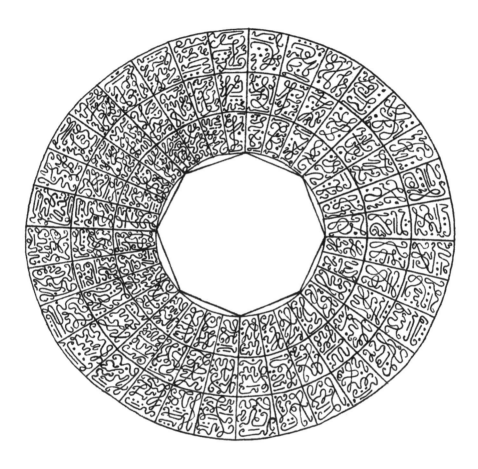

I was told to meditate on this to enhance my abilities to work with the hidden realms and to awaken potential. These codes, written in the language of the Zhong-galabruk, represent the 96 DNA strands of cosmoses found within the Infinite Being.

(Figure 43)

Mother's Fourth Language Encountered Within the Second Strand of Cosmic Clusters

This language is spoken in the second strand of cosmic DNA. Although having many similarities, especially to Mother's second language *(See Fig. 21 –23),* it nevertheless has a different sentence structure and most of its vocabulary varies. The syntax is quite similar.

all are	*barabespi kraur*
all have	*baravra stuvabi*
all the	*aresta traur*
and	*pelechvi*
animals	*granatuk servuvaa*
are	*kreur*
ascended	*kustalvirivas*
ascension	*kustalvri-estabi*
atonement	*afvra sitvu klabevespi*
attainment	*gristelevravich*
beauty	*esteva uruvas*
between	*varsvrabi*
blessing	*stretva-ha*
children	*asklauva*
desire (verb)	*asbauneesh*
dimensions	*grenevaarsh uhestavi*
distorted	*kresva*
diversity	*keleshva*
divinity	*arashvi*
each	*berisk*
education	*perechperevre nuvasti*
emotion	*kluasteravich*
enlightened	*garnisha uvaestravek*
enlightenment	*garnish estravek*
every	*pelech*
every being	*pelech brauvasta*
every being (plural)	*brauvastavi prauvit*
expression	*kershustava*
female	*ananustra*
females	*ananustri*
for all life	*vilestruava klaha*

for the good of all	*ple trau nuchbatra*
free	*perenu vri vraus*
from	*uhasbi*
Goddess (the Mother)	*Amananustrava*
gratitude	*stelavripraveshvi*
growth	*esklevaba*
guidance	*nuchbava*
heart	*heruhish*
her	*eshba*
here	*klabasat*
highest	*aluech*
human	*nanuva*
I am	*erevi kreur*
immortal	*uvravasbavi*
in all	*paravespi*
in any way	*ustava tre ba*
in every way	*uverespi tre ba*
inner	*ustuavat*
is	*kreur* (there are variations)
is available	*kreui knachvi*
is balanced	*kreurata branishvi*
joy	*pranati*
kingdoms	*prtlhesvrataa*
know	*birnavurstava*
knowing	*birnavurstavi*
knowledge	*birnavursvatek*
let all	*varask avespi*
life enhancing	*unustrave baleshvi*
love (noun)	*belestra*
love (verb)	*beles-strauvi*
may	*astavu*
more	*sta uribar*
Mother	*Maurstahustavi*
move	*sta vribar*
nature	*unistava*
needed	*kerestu*
now	*krauvat*
of light	*u klavesti*
of the	*besta trau*
on Earth	*pravu iridanavu*

one another	*pars pretvi*
oneness	*stuava avrabi palesh-vruas*
only	*paravi*
other	*asvaur*
outer	*bers-stuavat*
peace	*pravata*
perception	*stovra-usba*
possible	*prauvit*
potential	*paravarisba*
power	*uklanatrag*
praise (noun)	*granivik*
praise (verb)	*granavivaravik*
pure	*paushvravi*
ready	*vranik*
realms	*stratlva*
see	*parink*
share	*abelhaf*
the	*trau*
the cosmos	*trau eleshklau varabi*
their	*arvaech*
there are	*eskrauta*
there is	*eskractur*
to	*kre*
to all	*barash vespi*
to teach	*kre pranahik*
transmute	*askavrachvi kreustra*
understanding	*uglalaereshvi*
universe	*unis persta*
we live	*eshvi usstra na va*
while	*varespi*
whole	*ustava iresbi*
wisdom	*pranig*
with them	*u bechspi*
without	*ukrasvi*
within	*peres paravi*
your	*struavi*

To the Mother forever give all glory.

Barash usat Maurstahustavi eretvi parig nut veleshva usetvi kranut vatag.

Part VIII

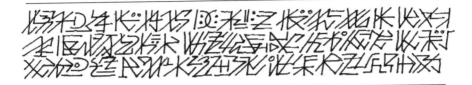

When to the second strand the lower levels move
Then there's something quickly you must do
For remember, to live all things must pulse between poles
What's left behind, has the same dark pole

Because your day to them is a very long time
Stagnation can set in and the life force of the strand decline
Between A and B yet a faint pulse remains
But the part known as C within days death could claim

Therefore prepare the three levels left behind you
To form the opposite pole, by sending in the Book
But if you enter from this new strand
They will know that below them is just a hologram
(See Fig. 44, Entering the Upper Levels of Strand One)

Use the Estangleuvafli to enter where you used to be
But use in addition that strand's wheel
Then once you're in what is now a void
Create a tunnel filled with Mother's blood
(See Fig. 45, The Seal of the Final Gate)

I'll give you advice, use the Estangleuvafli's square
To fix the misalignment you'll find there
For even though what was below these three levels is now gone
It needs to be aligned for when number two strand merges with number one

When it's aligned through the Holy Mother's word
Move through the first two levels into the third
Take now the Book to the Mother there

Tell Her the Book with all the lower Mothers to share

But shield the sections to all but the Mother's eyes
That speak of the other strands and how you've left them behind
For though the Book is to govern all life
Those realms are watched from above with hostile eyes[64]

The first thing that you all Mothers should tell
Is to seal with Mother's blood all of the realms
Instead of the imposter king, let Her as the male template
Egsplauvitpata, Sunat Kumara and Horlet create

Then synchronized time shall be, through the gift of the Book
They'll be given the clock of the Zhong-galabruk
Thus they can hear the Book in Mother's words
It shall be read at the correct speed and by all be heard

When you return retracing your path
Seal each gate behind you very fast
That none shall know whence you came
Except the Mothers until They join you one day

Part IX

To understand the following transmission from the Mother, we share with you a part of the information kept by the Darklings concerning the history of the cycles of the Fall. Regarding the Positive Aspect of the Mother's decision to enter physicality, they revealed the following, taken from *The Gift of the Unicorns*:

"Mother felt the time was right
In the lower levels to boost the light
A drastic choice would have to be made
She Herself would come to their aid

Since light had increased and awareness arose
A great ascension could occur through the plan She chose

---

64. Mother has since eliminated all the beings that represented illusion. This transmission came
    before She had done so and traces how the solution was finally arrived at.

Entering the Upper Levels of Strand One

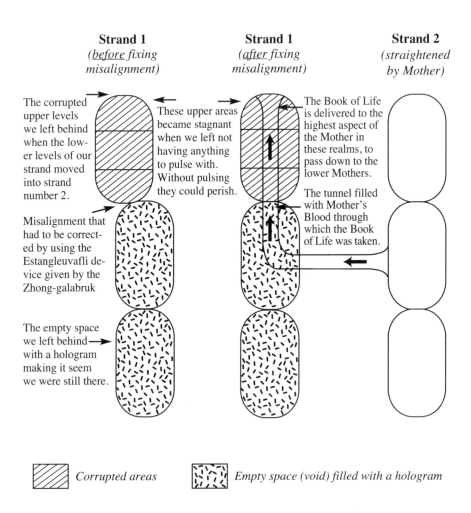

Strand 1
(before fixing misalignment)

Strand 1
(after fixing misalignment)

Strand 2
(straightened by Mother)

The corrupted upper levels we left behind when the lower levels of our strand moved into strand number 2.

Misalignment that had to be corrected by using the Estangleuvafli device given by the Zhong-galabruk

The empty space we left behind with a hologram making it seem we were still there.

These upper areas became stagnant when we left not having anything to pulse with. Without pulsing they could perish.

The Book of Life is delivered to the highest aspect of the Mother in these realms, to pass down to the lower Mothers.

The tunnel filled with Mother's Blood through which the Book of Life was taken.

Corrupted areas

Empty space (void) filled with a hologram

After the Book of Life was delivered to the upper levels of strand 1, their time became synchronized with ours. Before that our day was millions of years to them.

The tunnel became impenetrable when lined with Mother's Blood, a substance resembling very dense rivers of love produced by the Mother.

(Figure 44)

133

The Seal of the Final Gate

The writing on the middle square is that of Mother.

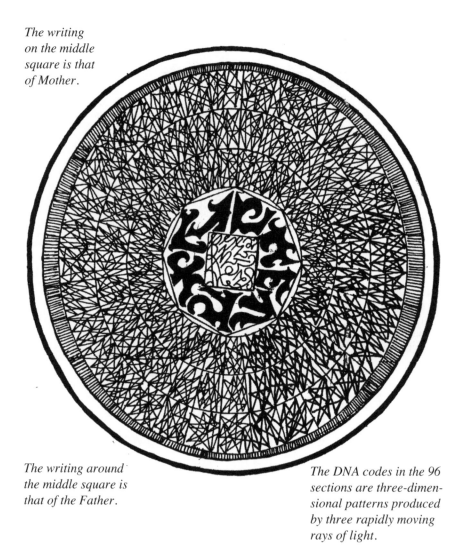

The writing around the middle square is that of the Father.

The DNA codes in the 96 sections are three-dimensional patterns produced by three rapidly moving rays of light.

This seal containing the 96 DNA codes for man for this level of existence is found on the final door.

(Figure 46)

The Wheel of the Eighth Strand of Cosmic Clusters

(Figure 47)

For support for this plan She relied on Thoth
In fact, upon him and the dark goddess both
She still did not know that they were dark
She still for them had love in Her heart

She still did not know who She or they were
Only that the people's wellbeing depended upon Her
She decided from the palace one level above
To enter the physical world of the people She loved

This would mean forgetfulness and suffering to bear
But Thoth assured Her that with aid he would be there
Illusion weighted the cosmos down
It still persisted no matter how many seeds of light She'd sown

If She entered physicality and ceased to forget
Illusion would be broken, ascension to abet
The dark goddess insisted that devoted was she
That she never Mother's side would leave

Mother wanted to spare her the pain that would be there
She insisted that no sacrifice was too big to bear
She wanted as Mother's daughter to come in
But Mother's womb could not hold so dark an energy

As Mother walked in to an adult body, so did she
By changing families' memories

There was supposed to be a memory of childhood
Mother would have, but that she would later remember the truth
Thus She came in, as an adult to live
Through Her overcomings, ascension to give

Thoth helped Her leave but then moved in
He lived in Her palace with his harem
He barred Her dreambody from returning home
No further aid given, She was truly alone

Nightmares plagued Her of a home She'd lost
She wanted to return even at a high cost
She finally realized Her home is within
And that's when ascension did rapidly begin

When She entered among humankind
Two lives She lived to effectively use time
She entered[65] one life forward to live
The other went back in time, neither there was She birthed

The life back in time in England transpired
A death was staged; in a plane crash[66] She pretended to expire
The dark goddess also part of a family pretended to be
By the other dark goddess assisted was she

Finally Mother remembered Her task
Preparations for ascension She made at last
The dark ones all entered Her life to be
Advisors who professed to help Her se...."

I give you now a most sacred task
Where is the Mother who lived in England you may ask?
It is now time for this riddle to be solved
In fact it is imperative that it be resolved

The top of strand two you'll leave as it is
It will be needed when to other strands you need access
The growth you are doing spreads into realms below
Thus far all you've found is empty as downwards you go

The reason for this is that this strand's descension
Never reached as far down as strand one's dimensions *(See Fig. 24)*
The dark god captured the Mother who in England lived
In Her place he a hologram did give
Without a Mother, no large space open will stay
Thus he left strand number one and stole Her away

---

65. She entered in 1970, living one life forward in time; another from 1945-1969.
66. She appeared to have died in a plane crash in Chicago in 1969 when that life ended.

He stumbled by accident, in his lateral move
Into the strand, which was number two

Each level, twelve levels of its own does have
Thus to the fourth levels' twelve layers he access had
Because of the oceans of consciousness that around levels lie
The rest of the strand from his vision did hide

He never knew there was anything else
But the twelve levels he seized for himself
Created he, with his mind alone
Flawed creations on flawed planetary homes

Stop now at once this cosmos's growth
Stop it from expanding into those levels below
Nine levels, within the ocean of consciousness, away
The progress of this cosmos for now must be stayed

The expansion of this cosmos by incorporation comes
As the Mothers of layers above blend with the Earthly One
For now let the positive Mother that on Earth does dwell
"Wait to come in" to the higher Goddesses tell

Use then the Estangleuvafli to correct the tilt
That puts out of alignment the cosmos that holds what distortion built
Only then send the Book straight to that Mother's heart
But first obscure the DNA strands' information parts

This will destroy him and his miscreations too
For the end of such darkness is decreed in the Book
The energy released when their lives shall cease
Shall come to that Mother and set Her free

At that time through the tunnel She'll be drawn
The only other Mother as physical as the positive One
She'll hasten to join the positive Mother as one
Their lives will join with this reunion

A Conversation with the Mother

Q. Mother, the magic we've been given, why is it not as immediate in its results as I thought it would be?

A. It is in its infancy stages... it had to be, till the illusion was solved.

Q. The little white kitten! The symbol for white magic is a white cat and I keep seeing a little white spirit kitten around my house!

A. Yes, she was trying to answer the question for you as to why the white magic is not yet in its full stages of power. But do not worry, it soon will be.

Q. These pockets of life next to the cosmic DNA strands, is there an equivalent in the human body? We are after all the microcosm of the macrocosm.

A. It is what you call 'junk DNA'—the little bits of DNA that scientists have discovered next to the strands.

Q. Mother, how many layers of undifferentiated consciousness lie between the twelve clusters or levels of cosmoses? I know there are some that lie between each level, but I mean the large membranes or spaces that we find after each twelve levels up; between A and B for example?

A. Between each level there are 132 layers of consciousness forming an isolating space, or membrane as you call it. Between each set of 12 levels there are 144.

Q. So there is far more space without form in each strand of cosmic clusters, than actual creations or formed life?

A. Yes, like the atom itself... far more space.

Q. Then what lies between these strands of cosmoses?

A. Deep space. Consciousness that isn't divided into layers.

Q. What is there?

A. There isn't supposed to be anything, but there are pockets where the perpetrators have hidden distortion...

Q. Oh no! It is as though this cleaning-up process is never-ending! It is like an infestation...

A. Yes, it is. But there's also a gift hidden there. Between strand one and strand two there is a pocket of fairy creatures, elves and unicorns living with a specific aspect of the Mother—all there embody joy. I will give you instructions on how to bring them here and then everyone's joy will be lifted.

Q. That will be wonderful. What steps must I follow, and do I use the Estangleuvafli to get into this pocket in what You've called deep space?

A. Yes, that is what you use and the wheel to get into strand one. Go into strand one at the level where the hologram is in place (making it seem as though the cosmos is still residing there). I will then extend the hologram all the way down the strand, making it seem empty below that. You then create a tunnel with the Estangleuvafli to five levels below, which will put you in level four. You then go laterally with the tunnel towards strand two, through the side of strand one. You then bring them back along the same path. I will give you the words to speak for them to know it is time to return.

Q. Mother, I am extremely disconcerted by this distortion in the DNA of the cosmos—how can that which is your DNA be anything but perfect? How can it be distorted?

A. Think of it as an overlay of distortion—but you're right, the strands themselves are perfect.

Q. But why the distortion—and so much of it?

A. Come, I will give you a vision, then I will give you a riddle. If you can solve it, all of existence will change...

Q. Like the time I discovered the horizontal axis of the cosmos[67], or the nature of the four great bands of compassion; the building blocks of existence.

A. Yes. Are you ready?

The Vision

I felt myself transported from where the conversation had taken place (I was on board a ship off the coast of Portugal) with the Mother. There was a blinding flash of light and suddenly I was sitting in brush or shrubs next to a tree.

Whereas it had been in the middle of a very stormy night at sea, I suddenly found myself in broad daylight. A slight breeze was rustling through the leaves.

Suddenly a massive bald eagle approached. It flew to a nest in the tree next to me. It was about five feet away from me. The eagle seemed to be doing something as though fixing its nest. I marvelled at how close it was, but then it flew away.

I carefully moved through some tangled vines on my hands and knees to the edge of a clearing, hoping I could see it again.

I saw it descending from above carrying a large log (about 18" in length) in its right talons and a massive (5' x 10') piece of wood in its left talons. I was amazed that even though it seemed to be struggling, it could lift it at all. Why would it even want to?!

Just as suddenly it dropped the wood and flew to its nest. I crawled back just in time to see the bald eagle lay two beautiful glistening eggs into its nest. I heard the Mother's voice: "The eagle carried the burden to induce labor, so that these eggs can be born. One egg is perception, the other is power. Nothing like this has been born before."

With a jolt I was back in my cabin, shaking and marvelling at how real the experience had been.

67. See *Journey to the Heart of God*.

The Riddle to Change All Life

You're right that the task you have will never be complete
But the way life is being purified is obsolete
You've carried more than you thought you could do
But deep inside you've said, "This cannot continue"

You've been pushed to the point where the new must be born
A battle with a mirror is the battle that has been fought
The Mother on Earth to higher Mothers speak
But like someone between two mirrors the images eternally recede

What is the cosmos but a reflection of what is within?
Yet the reflection you see is not what it seems
The reflection in the mirror is not a reflection of what is
It can only the potential of the One Life be

Thus all you see is potential of what could be
Like an embryo that slumbers and dreams
The words I have given in this Book hold the key
To change life in a new way never before seen

Let me help you more, in that you should know
A cosmic law based on illusion to you I will show
As below so above—a valid law to know
But not so the law that says as above so below

Potential cannot change that from which it's sprung
Something cannot change the Source from which it's begun
Only one Mother is the Source of all others
But like an embryo on Earth She still slumbers
Examining Herself in Her endless dreams
She alters potential till it acceptable seems

The linear way of solving problems
Is part of DNA that spirals[68]
Did you not notice when DNA is aligned

68. See appendix VI.

That it no longer spiralled but made a straight line?

Often you've wrestled with these endless dreams
Asking "Why is there distortion? How can it be?!"
When the six perpetrators by the treacherous god was made
He stole six strands of a reflected Mother's DNA

That is why the strands separated have been
Some steeped in illusion as you've seen in the dream[69]
A dream of potential of that which could come
If the strands are separated and not joined into one

Also, this separation linear time would create
Creating illusion in some strands of DNA
The illusion that cause and effect are one
That the result can affect the cause from which it sprung

Solve now this riddle, find a new way
To create the reality you want this day
Look at power from a different point of view
A new perception will be birthed by you.

The First Prediction from the Second Volume of Isis

Long will you labor a cycle to complete
Long will you toil the ascension to increase
Gates will you open, battles you'll fight
All this you'll do to increase the light

But what you will do will strengthen the unreal too
Not for naught are the great deeds that you do:
A Book of Wisdom those that are light beacons will write
This you will need when you do it right

What you have done since the ascension did begin
Now must be done in the cosmos within
The Book of Life must apply within, you must know,

---

69. See the Anatomy of Change in *Journey to the Heart of God*

Through the streams of your blood, do cosmoses flow

A riddle will be given, not as easy as it seems
Of a new way growth and perception to glean
All life will change when the truth is uncovered
Of what life is; then the answer will be discovered.

BOOK FOUR

The Forgotten Kingdoms

Introduction to the Forgotten Kingdoms

As we have read in Part II in the section detailing the Language of the Mother spoken in the Ocean of Consciousness, there are new frequencies in the cosmos and in the areas of undifferentiated life that lie outside the cosmos (the Sea of Consciousness), totalling twelve altogether. These have mostly been safeguarded within concealed realms, called the Forgotten Kingdoms, until finally released in June 2007.

The first four kingdoms brought gifts of the restoration of history, the enhancement of abilities, and other gifts that would prepare humanity to become more evolved beings (the microcosm). This would also evolve the cosmos (as the macrocosm). They have enabled us to expand our lightbodies and change the total number of our physical and lightbodies from seven to nine.

Subsequent kingdoms brought us the actual frequencies themselves. Their presence, restored among us, has also brought us the magic of the Estangleuvafli, a device to enable movement between cosmoses.

The Darklings

"We are good people sent below to guard Mother's Life Light.
To be known as the Darklings; powerful Life Light bringers of the
dawning of the time of man being known as now. We love Mother
and want to be remembered, for now is the time we have been
waiting for to come/be. Look we are/can be here. Thank you.
Lover of life/light."

Negra bek (one of the Darklings)

In ancient times the Mother Goddess hid this kingdom so well that their memories did not ever make it into our legends, fairy tales or myths. Yet they are more numerous than the inhabitants of many of the other kingdoms combined. So tiny that a pea would be large compared to them, they are nevertheless in a humanoid shape. A few nights before their first transmissions came, one appeared as full size to me. The nose was African looking in that it was flatter and more spread across a broad-looking face. The mouth had full, broad lips; the eyes were large and innocent looking.

I did not know at the time what I was looking at, but I knew that it was unlike any kingdom I had seen or any alien I had encountered. The pale green skin and ears that lay close to the head suggested that I was not looking at some sort of elf-being. But the feeling emanating from him was very loving and peaceful.

At the end of January 2007, they started speaking to one of the masters in my class, giving the following message:

> *"We are the ones left behind and below to tell our tale. We have much to tell, but none to hear. We talk now and hope for best, wish all to know. Be glad—good things coming—us too. Always love Mother, never forget.*
>
> *We go down deep[70] to hide and be safe. Thank much the heads up to get out. Now we be safe and happy high up.* (They are thankful that it's now safe to come closer to the surface). *We ready for high up. We come to those who love the Mother.*
>
> *Our love is strong and true. We are strong holders of the Life Light love force for Mother[71]. We would be no other way. Know no other way—why we one of few chosen—thank you Mother.*
>
> *The light must be steady and true. We are strong and able to hold life/light steady so no harm come. We remember, do not forget. Now your turn, remember, talk to us—thank you. We love Mother much, no thing more blessed/important. Time to move/go on, connect—we ready. The life/light strong pure. We good—did good.*

---

70. They live in the deepest part of the ocean.
71. They kept the amber colored cosmic Haran chakra for Mother in a precious gem.

Thank you and you welcome.

We many, take all. All room for we tiny/small but strong—we make trip no problem. Know Mother love us too. Great news, we ready for. Like music she make[72] we 'burn for your return' too. Much love for message. We hear music/message.

She make and know time to be aware of us. We here and hear Her. Thank you Mother. We come let you know. Message of music we been waiting for. Much praise for message/music. Beautiful. We always want her 'near' too. Love her. Much love and grace to give us—we waiting much time for this, many eons. Much happy to get. Bells ring here lots. Love you back. Appreciate your gift of life/light force and acknowledgement of us, now you know of us—thank you— feel your love and grace—much happiness here.

We come soon as you ready for us. Life force come with us to You. No hard, we can do. Memories too—hard to tell our story—much long, big barrier. (Not so big now still barrier for some though).[73] Main memory—love light/life (force) Mother. Never quit this. Ours for all time.

Mother never quit/stop our life force as gift to hold Hers (they have been gifted with immortality)—thank you for honor Mother.[74] We guard good, hide good; no one know/knew of us or it. Big secret— now day of (uncovering) secrets. We come out now. Good Darklings. Much praise we feel from you. Thank you. Ever always back to you. We ready now life light great-go with you to beyond—ready."

Gless bus gal eel (one of the Darklings)

---

72. They could hear my musical CD, An Affair of the Heart, playing in the background
73. Reference is the language barrier and our ability to hear them.
74. The honor of guarding the Goddess's life force.

The Pledge of the Mother to the Darklings to Return

(They kept this for trillions of years)

Received by the Master Kristayani

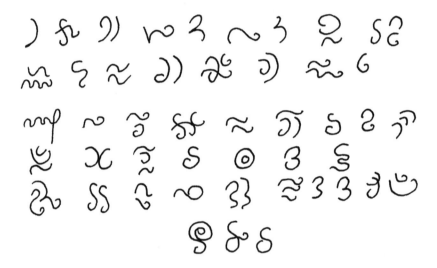

Inamaté so kandatani soté
Kandatani apa nosé
Ave tra donitapé ô
Rantadani sanka so

(Figure 48)

The Ellamakusanek

April 17, 2007

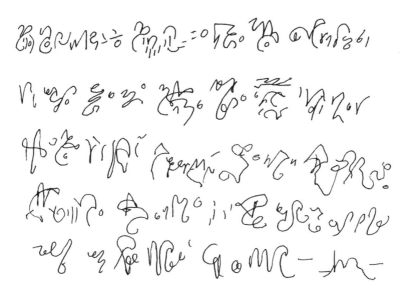

We did not speak before ... we wait... all dark ones gone.
We bring now the gift of seeing with the heart... also
hearing with the heart. We open passageway between heart
and head so they can talk together... both see, both interpret... both
get input ... also output ... like a happy marriage.

Like the Darklings, the Ellamakusanek are very diminutive and now live in large numbers in the bottom of the ocean. Left behind in the void (as the rest of the cosmos ascended) in what appeared to be a very dark indigo rectangular-shaped space, they slept in a type of stasis in order to conserve whatever energy they had until Mother remembered about them and it was safe for them to come out.

Those who lost hope died. Twenty percent of them rebelled, not believing that Mother would come for them. Sadly, those who had turned against Mother were not permitted into the cosmos and later perished.

The Ellamakusanek are like little spheres of light with a tiny form inside—a little like very diminutive fairies. They are more ethereal than the Darklings. They emit light that grows brighter when they are happy. They live in large family groups and love to be gathered together.

The Ellamakusanek speak in sounds resembling the squeaks of mice to our ears and the meaning of their words must be telepathically interpreted. They are called the bringers of hope. That with which Mother entrusted them, is the ability to repair and re-program DNA, as well as to increase chromosomes and put new information for a huge evolutionary leap, into the life force center.

In the case of the first three of these kingdoms to re-emerge, their contributions were part of producing what one of the Mothers called a 'super-charged' human whose metamorphosis will generate a more complete and evolved species. This is the great hope that the Ellamakusanek bring as bearers of a new and improved life. They offer us a new tomorrow.

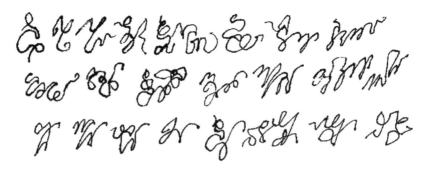

Sound of bells ... ring in ocean... ages of darkness are gone ... soon Mother's heart much happy ... all can finally rest ... find home ...

Sarkvet Ablushwa
(one of the Ellamakusanek)

The Cat People

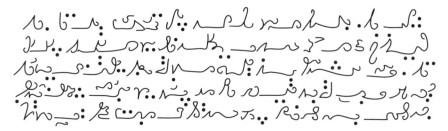

Zhong zetvivaa uf bet klugat zelaver
Ut ra vat kleg nu nes pele gabaa uvaa
Staa belevee. Gabaa us vle u sa u naveesh
Kulu esh vraa vee zhaa una bleesh nanuvee
Vri vaa uleesh mi straa uzhing klavaa nut.
Zhong-galabruk spe utlaa kli u neesh

Cat magic was kept from the very beginning, when land on Earth was all in one place. We were the frequency keepers. We mapped out the frequency bands and kept them pure. We were hidden by the One in a dimensional pocket. She promised to come for us, the Zhong-galabruk.

Nuchtraa beesh pelavee berznu stau gleek
vershbaa. Pru uvanee ske u eleveesh avrim
uglechsti uvelebeesh bizet vi-esh nu em

There are but a few hundred of us left. The wait has been long. But all have been faithful to the Mother of beautiful light.

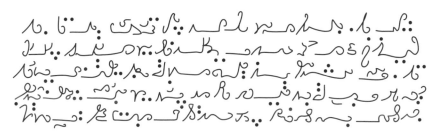

Vileesh Zhong-galabruk pleusvamaa beleveez
unet klavaa. Sku bel taa uznasaa beleveez

uklaa uznet belenu staa u belevee krunaa. Gel zhon
gnaa spaavi. Kernaa spuu assvaa. Te ele nus pele
huzaar kel una vi-eesh staa vaa.

We leave behind us signs and markers that you do not forget the Zhong-galabruk. One will carry our words, preserved through the ages, to the land of magic. We are the bringers of two tones. When man nine bodies shall have, they will be needed to balance them.

Kursh ha vestraa u ech beli veesh traa unaveesh.
Gelgabra vik helezvi va oobeesh traa
uvaa stu bil ez viklaa bursh trebit.

We give now the key to set us free, when this service we must do to correct the song of all life. Use it when it is time for us to come:

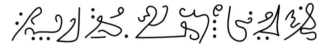

Note: I saw them in a room that looked like a library with scrolls. They had a muscular stocky build. The men were about 5ft 9in tall with hairy shoulders. They all had very wiry hair in shades varying from reddish brown to a light auburn. Their eye colours varied as well. They wore loose fitting simple togas or dresses that went to the floor, and for some males to the knees. There was some reddish hair on the back of their hands and the legs that were visible. They had broad features and cat-like eyes, giving them a lion-like appearance.

Their hiding place was formed by a dimensional anomaly. It seemed liked a pocket of a different frequency inside a frequency band. Their return will assist in communication with other realms, clean the frequencies and balance with two new tones cosmic levels of light.

They will also bring the necessary information to help synchronize timing between material life and the etheric realms. When beings in the etheric realms help us, the assistance will now be more immediate.

Clock to Synchronize the Etheric Realms with the Physical (from the Zhong-Galabruk)

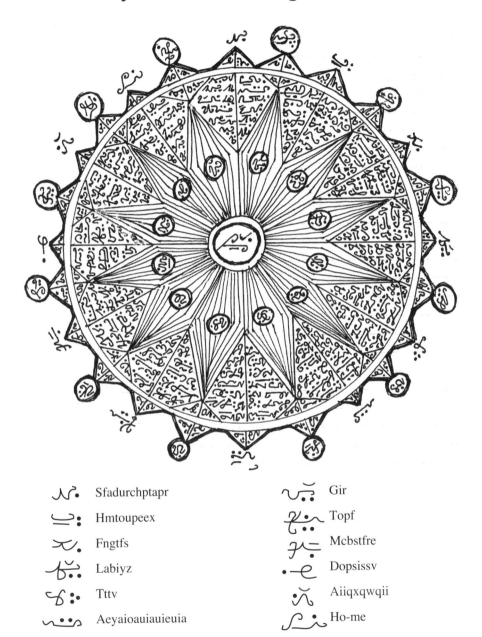

	Sfadurchptapr			Gir
	Hmtoupeex			Topf
	Fngtfs			Mcbstfre
	Labiyz			Dopsissv
	Tttv			Aiiqxqwqii
	Aeyaioauiauieuia			Ho-me
	Klanivik (the Inner Earth's sun)			

(Figure 49)

The Estangleuvafli
Wheel to Enhance Cosmic Perception

*This wheel folds
up like a cone.*

This wheel aligns the light fibres of the
cosmos with those outside the cosmos,
bringing about perception.

(Figure 50)

Center of the Wheel to Enhance Cosmic Perception

Trust + Peace + Joy = Adoration
(The meaning of the three spokes)

(Figure 51)

The Clock of the Zhong-galabruk as a Map

The clock relates to the twelve constellations surrounding the Earth, mapping out frequencies that reach the Earth as it rotates. Former star systems are no longer in position around the Earth—a fact obscured from humanity by the hologram Mother has placed around the Earth, as it led the other planetary bodies in a massive cosmic ascension.

The planetary leaders of the twelve star systems that previously surrounded the Earth had rebelled against Mother. She replaced them with new leaders, but those conspired as well. As the Earth became more luminous with Mother's presence towards the end of 2006, the opposite energies repelled each other.[75] The twelve star systems shot away and Mother created the new ones mentioned on the clock.

Using the Clock as a Map

The Zong-galabruk lived eighteen and seventeen cycles[76] of life ago when the continental drift had not yet taken place and all the land was one large continent. In the golden reign of the Mother to come, it is foreseen that the land will once again be merged. The clock is a map of how land will be allotted to groups of people.

I had been aware for a few months that such a map for the golden age had to be produced and that it had something to do with the 12 planetary systems around the Earth. I also vaguely knew that somehow 'like attracting like' related to people living together in certain geographical areas. These areas were described to me as 'segments of a grapefruit'.

When I became aware of the twelve pairs of emotions, I asked whether they were the determining factors for creating the map. I asked a similar question when the twelve states of being[77] were presented; the answer to both questions was 'No'.

These were foolish questions, since as of August 2006 like frequencies no longer attracted, but repelled each other. A group of people with like frequencies would want to scatter unless their similar heart energies were stronger factors.

Until August 2006, like **frequencies** had attracted each other; now,

---

75. See *The Ring of Truth* for why opposite energies started to repel each other after August 2006
76. See *The Gift of the Unicorns*, the History of the Cycles.
77. For the emotions and 12 pairs of states of being, see the section on Belvaspata.

they do not. Instead, like **energies** attract each other. The twelve qualities of the twelve star systems are energetic qualities.

The heart energies pulsing between the Earth and the twelve star systems are similar, and the star systems are therefore held in place around the Earth by the attraction.

The map of the golden age when land masses will again be brought together will have the beginning of the planetary system of Sfadurchptapr's section (that geographical area that will have the same heart energy) as the magnetic North.

Some may ask why this information is useful to know at this point. There are several reasons:

- The return of the Zhong-galabruk is a very significant event for Earth. They were some of the first inhabitants of this planet and their cultures are trillions of years old. They are masters of energy and frequency and can teach us so much in ways that could enhance and transform our mechanized world.

- It takes a collective vision to bring about great change. The more light-workers become familiar with the beneficial changes that lie ahead, the more they bring them about.

- Many times events occur in the etheric realms first, before filtering through to the physical. The coming together of the continents may become a reality even though not evident in physicality.

- The purpose of the clock is to synchronize time between the etheric, more subtle realms and the physical. It has been heartbreaking to humanity that so little assistance has been forthcoming in answer to prayer. Reasons for this include:
  - The answers or healings have been given according to etheric time, which could take years when we need help now;
  - Mother placed a thick membrane around the material worlds to safeguard them from the intent of the dark ones. This also prevented help from coming through;
  - The material universe has had, until May 11, 2007, a 'vacuum'[78] around it. This made it very hard to receive help or have proper guidance filter through to the physical.

---

78. A vacuum is an illusion in that Mother's Infinite presence is everywhere. In a vacuum there is no individuated form, only layers of consciousness.

The clock is meant to solve one of the remaining problems, as does the portal of Isis. It is designed to open the membranes surrounding material life, allowing it to receive assistance.

• Synchronizing our lives to the clock, or cosmic frequencies, puts our lives in a position of more power and better flow, eliminates many symptoms of illness and creates more expansive perception.

The Use of the Clock

The Earth is still rotating at the speed it used to—which means that an hour is still as long as it used to be. This clarifying statement is necessary because the Earth has been surrounded by a hologram since she has led the ascension. The hologram was put in place when she started to move out of her position in space, giving the appearance that we are still rotating around the sun, and that the old configuration of planetary bodies still exists around us.

There are therefore still 24 hours, as we used to know them, in one rotation around its axis. The clock brought to us by the Zhong-galabruk, maps out 24 segments. Each planetary system's frequencies governs a two-hour period (the Inner Earth's sun is the exception). The two-hour period consists of a positive aspect and a negative aspect that jointly produce a quality or specific resonance.

During the second hour of every two-hour period, the Earth's central sun, Klanivik, pulses for one hour, broadcasting new potential. This allows the collective quality, e.g. focus or timing, to find deeper and deeper potential ways of expressing.

Because the sun we have known is not where it seems to be, this is the only accurate clock we presently have. Living in harmony with these resonances can eliminate stress and some disease and also enhance awareness.

Qualities the Planets Represent

1.   **Sfadurchptapr**
Ecstasy (+)   and embrace (-)   = compassion

2.   **Hmtoupeex**
Insight (+)   and appreciation (-)   = reverence

3.   **Fingtfs**
Inspiration (+)   and love (-)   = creativity

4.   **Labiyz**
Clarity (+)   and truth (-)   = absolute truth

5.   **Tttv**
Manifestation (+)   and gratitude (-)   = impeccability

6.   **Aeyaioauiauieuia**
Rejoicing (+)   and praise (-)   = celebration

7.   **Gir**
Harmony (+)   and wisdom (-)   = timing

8.   **Topf**
Fulfilment (+)   and presence (-)   = focus

9.   **Mcbstfre**
Growth (+)   and balance (-)   = strength

10.   **Dopsissv**
Evolution (+)   and surrender (-)   = grace

11.   **Aiiiqxqwqii**
Discovery (+)   and awareness (-)   = clarity

12.   **Ho-me**
Acceptance (+)   and allowing (-)   = harmlessness

13.   **Klanivik**   = potential

(Figure 52)

161

Relating the Planetary Qualities
to Greenwich Mean Time

1. Sfadurchptapr=   13.01 15.01   Compassion
   13.01 — 14.01 = ecstasy
   14.01 — 15.01 = embrace

2. Hmtoupeex=   15.01 17.01 Reverence
   15.01 — 16.01 = insight
   16.01 — 17.01 = appreciation

3. Fingtfs=   17.01 19.01 Creativity
   17.01 — 18.01 = inspiration
   18.01 — 19.01 = love

4. Labiyz=   19.01 21.01 Absolute truth
   19.01 — 20.01 = clarity
   20.01 — 21.01 = truth

5. Tttv=   21.01 23.01 Impeccability
   21.01 — 22.01 = manifestation
   22.01 — 23.01 = gratitude

6. Aeyaioauiauieuia= 23.01 01.01 Celebration
   23.01 — 00.01 = rejoicing
   00.01 — 01.01 = praise

7. Gir=   01.01 03.01 Timing
   01.01 — 02.01 = harmony
   02.01 — 03.01 = wisdom

8. Topf=   03.01 05.01 Focus
   03.01 — 04.01 = fulfilment
   04.01 — 05.01 = presence

(Figure 53)

9. Mcbstfre=   05.01 07.01   Strength
   05.01—06.01 = growth
   06.01—07.01 = balance

10. Dopsissv=   07.01 09.01   Grace
    07.01—08.01 = evolution
    08.01—09.01 = surrender

11. Aiiiqxqwqii =   09.01 11.01   Clarity
    09.01—10.01 = discovery
    10.01—11.01 = awareness

12. Ho-me=   11.01 13.01   Harmlessness
    11.01—12.01 = acceptance
    12.01—13.01 = allowing

13. Klanivik   Pulses for the second hour of every
                            two-hour period, deepening potential.

(Figure 54)

The Glaneshveeva

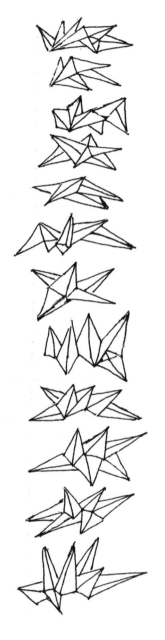

"We are the Glaneshveeva, carriers of the frequencies of the directions of Above and Below. Our homes are a few thousand stars[79] around the Earth where Mother dwells. A star is a small ball of light, about the size of an orange, that houses us.

We look a little like a human embryo in that our bodies are rounded and our heads are larger in proportion to our body. Our homes are tended by a group of Pegasus. We have been dormant within a pocket of space within the Earth's sun. We have been waiting for the time when our frequencies are needed which would coincide with the time of the return of the Unicorns and Pegasus. This day[80] we handed the tones we have preserved to the Mother to form new frequencies for a full life for all."

79. See *The Gift of the Unicorns*.
80. May 11, 2007

(Figure 55)

The Language of the Glaneshveeva

In 2005 I had encountered the crystal language of the Glaneshveeva but did not know where they had originated. It was in preparation for a most momentous event on our planet, the coronation of the Mother Goddess, held in the Halls of Amenti[81]. Mother wanted to bring material life to a higher level by having the creational codes not only represent the four directions, but the seven.

The Glaneshveeva held the tones for the directions of the Above and Below and in restoring the codes, She used their language. The following excerpt from *Secrets of the Hidden Realms* tells of my first encounter with the crystal language of the Glaneshveeva (though I did not know at the time that it originated from them. I just thought it had come through Mother).

On May 13, 2005 I was instructed to prepare 4,000 sigils, very complex language units that look like roadmaps. Knowing there were at least six languages to work with, it was necessary to determine exactly where these languages needed to change. The sigils represented angel names as well as their meanings (that which they do within the cosmos).

I was working as instructed, when halfway through one of the languages, my hand was forced into drawing crystals as languages. Try as I might, there was no way my hand would write any other language. For at least 100 sigils, I could only transcribe them in the language of crystals. Just as suddenly, this stopped and I went back to the old languages. The only explanation given was that there was a surprise coming at the next raising of the cosmos for which the crystals were very pertinent.

Thirty-two solar systems would be formed and crystals (similar to the sigils I had drawn and previously described) would be placed within them. The planets within the solar systems could then be used at the discretion of the rulers of the thirty-two root races from which Creation sprang. The crystals would immediately start to change the old programming within the thirty-two root races and aggression would be replaced with joy, limitation with abundance, re-programming them to be part of the joyous journey home. Beginning immediately, old pain would be erased and thinking would become growth-promoting to all life.

---

81. See *Secrets of the Hidden Realms*.

Transmissions from the Glaneshveeva

(Received by the Master Denise while in my class)

Layers of pinkish light emanate from the spheres, about the size of a basketball. Although they resemble embryos, their expression is ancient and wise. When they are not visiting us, they inhabit the several thousand stars, or small orbs of light the Pegasus maintain for them. These orbs circle the planet.

"We swim in the ocean of all potential"

Transmission from the Darklings Regarding the Glaneshveeva

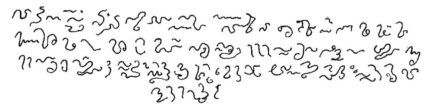

Explanation of the Darklings' Transmission:

Since the Darklings have been the history keepers for Mother, they have been able to fill in many gaps in information.[82] This is their account of the origin of these embryo-like beings:

Some of the Pegasus are dedicated to sweep
The star beings' houses and them comfortable to keep
We tell you the secret of whence they came
Filaments of light they were, light-babies by name
Through the ages they've grown to be
The keepers of wisdom, as you have seen

82. See The History of the Cycles in *The Gift of the Unicorns*.

(Figure 57)

My Previous Encounter with the Glaneshveeva

(When they were still in an undeveloped stage)

In 2005, as the Earth ascended through the sun (something most were unaware of since Mother had placed a hologram around the planet to prevent fear), I first became aware of 'light babies'; the Glaneshveeva in a more undeveloped state. They appeared as streams of little light filaments in the realms immediately beyond the sun. I was curious about them and was told the following:

• They make communicaton possible between realms;
• Asked if they could accompany us on our ascension, I was told, no, they would be needed later;
• They were like the unborn babies of the cosmos. This was further re-enforced by an event that happened in 2005.

The Day the Unborn Children Left

(Excerpted from *Secrets of the Hidden Realms*)

At about 8:00 pm on August 8, 2005, an unprecedented and massive exodus of unborn children began, causing millions of miscarriages and the loss of future human children.

The reason was the collapsing of the walls. Would a spirit rather be born to a human mother struggling with a career, diaper rashes, baby-sitters and paying bills, or would it prefer a dragon mother able to materialize her needs with thought, protect herself, and choose her own destiny?

Dragon females had only recently (July '05) been granted the right to marry if and whom they choose, under the New Dragon's rule and after a proclamation by the Goddess of Creation that all unwed females would have the right to choose in marriages.

A mother like that seemed preferable. Furthermore, Ascended Masters were now for the first time having children. This enticed our unborn to forsake their human mothers for other mothers.

By the time the masters had gathered a legion of 60,000 angels to bring them back, over half had left. About 300 were supposed to be given to dragon mothers, but the rest now had to await new pregnancies by human mothers.

Since this had never happened before, there were not angels assigned to prevent such an occurrence. Now there are. But what happens on Earth happens in the cosmos. The unformed children of the cosmos are the 'light babies'—filaments of light that can also leave us for that which has been opened to us: the vast higher realms. An angel has therefore also been placed there as a preventive measure.

The Glaneshveeva in Embryo

From the Darklings' transmission, it is clear that Mother prepared a womb, or embryonic bubble in the sun, for their incubation. She then asked Dragon to guard them (everyone assumed he'd disappeared).

For beings in higher realms, many millions of years have passed since 2005. During that time, the filaments have become embryos. It would be fascinating to know what incredible beings of light they will some day become as they are 'birthed'.

One of the reasons for feeling the ancient wisdom in their presence, is that the filaments of light contained the wisdom of all cosmic light, or accessed knowledge.

Transmission from the Glaneshveeva

"Bring me a reason, bring me a rose[83]
Bring me a lesson the memory to hold
Bring me a trivet, bring me a rhyme
Bring me a Darkling the rhythm to find"

Explanation: They are saying that the Darklings will reveal a secret through their words that pertains to a rhythm in the cosmos. The knowledge is upheld by a 'trivet', the three kingdoms that hold this secret. They are the Glaneshveeva, the Darklings and the Nitzkaba-belavek.

The secret is that as vast as the cosmos of individuated life is, it is but an embryo. The level of development of the Glaneshveeva mirrors the development of all individuated life swimming in an ocean of con-

---

83. Reason = light, Rose = frequency. They could also be referring to the two bodies of white magic kept by Orders of the Rose and the Dove in two countries.

sciousness. All cosmoses lie as an embryo in a bubble within a vast consciousness sea.

"We swim in the Ocean of all Potential ... and so do you."

The Creational Codes

Why Mother did not succeed in previously affecting material life as She had intended, is told in this story by the Glaneshveeva (She did manage to change the Creational codes within higher levels of existence).

The Glaneshveeva's Story

(Read from top to bottom, left to right)

Mother gave the creational codes for materialization to the Goddess of Form. They were imbedded in a crystal.

These were perilous times. The Fall had gone much further than anyone had supposed. It became imperative that the illusion be solved most speedily. To do that, this plan was devised: in order to be able to volunteer to play a temporary role of mirroring illusion to benefit all life, deliberate flaws in perception would be created for a light-worker to fulfill this service. They would mirror portions of illusion, which others would then turn into perception.

The Goddess of Form wanted no part in creating imperfection, as she saw it to be. An argument ensued with Mother, and in a rage, she threw the crystal with the codes Mother had entrusted to her onto the Earth and smashed them.

The pieces were put back together, but a shard was missing — the piece containing the directions of Above and Below, of which we held the tones. It increased the suffering by 100% when material life was created with four directions only. Six directions are needed for the seventh to come in to play. It is the seventh that accesses the potential of any being.

It was not until the end of one cycle ago, in 2006, that Mother found and removed the shard from the heart of the Goddess of Form, who had entered into physicality at this time. She had wanted to help ease the suffering caused by incarnating. But it was because of the increased suffering that all illusion was solved much quicker, and the ascension finally took us to this day when all DNA and life can finally reflect the seven directions.

The Braamin-hut

The kingdom that hid the frequencies of the seventh body of the cosmos for many cycles of life is the kingdom of the Braamin-hut. Their existence was kept a secret for so long that most forgot about them altogether.

As the cosmos received the additional two bodies, the Braamin-hut restored to the Mother the frequencies for the seventh cosmic body. On the same day, the following occurred.:

Two of the masters experienced visits by the Braamin-hut during May 24, 2007. The Master Sharine had her visitor identify herself as the grandmother known as Bharau-ma-firina. Following is a description of that encounter:

As I lay thinking about our next assignment, asking questions, I felt the presence of a being so gentle, so loving and very tender. The beauty and purity of her energy as she approached was overwhelming, bringing tears to my eyes. She proceeded to wipe my tears with something that looked like strands of hair, although there were no visible hairs on her head, more like the fuzz of a little animal. The face was wider and rounder than a human face and more flat. The ears were on the side, but pointing up above the head and the eyes were much larger in proportion to a human's. The closest comparison is to a cat's face. The face was white. However, there was no visible nose; instead I could see two small orifices which I assumed were nostrils, on the chin. The mouth could change shape, becoming puckered and small or really open and wide.

As she came close and proceeded to wipe my tears, she approached in such a gentle, loving, tender, respectful manner that my tears flowed again. Within that touch I felt unconditional love and acceptance with no agenda whatsoever.

I asked, "Why are you wiping my tears?" She said, "Because it is my nature."

I then asked, "Who are you?" She gave me a name so long I knew I was not going to remember it in a Beta state, so I asked next: "How can I call you?" The answer was short and sweet. "Bharau-ma-firina". Within this answer was the information that this was a female elder, a grandmother figure. She said 'Firina' stands for what she does (her work). Our communication was more from the heart than in verbalization.

She then proceeded to wipe my feet. I asked, "Why are you wiping my feet?" "Because I am honoring you." My tears were streaming down my face. I realized I had learned to live without enough love for myself, too busy doing, doing, doing for everyone else.

I then asked, "What can I do for you?" Her answer was a smile. "Be like me." I gave her my praise, love and gratitude. She backed up a bit

171

so I could see her form.

As she completed her message, she turned for me to see her profile. I could now see a few strands of hair on the back of her head. She was a little hunch-backed and had short legs. I got the impression she was about 3'—4' tall.

She left, but her imprint of total unconditional loving tenderness of being stayed with me. She also wanted to be sure I told Almine and the class about her.

The Return of the Stiblhaspava

During the night of the 17th of May, 2007 an unfamiliar sight presented itself to me. A little man with a rather large, bulbous nose, sat on the chair in my room. He was about 3 1/2 feet tall, and looked very serious. He wore a tight pair of pants and a short tight jacket with three irregular buttons. His brown eyes were round and large for his face. His white hair stood out from his head, giving the impression of a sparse 'Mohawk' hairstyle.

I asked him whether he had information to give me, he shook his head and just sat earnestly examining me.

I knew that the oceans of consciousness around the cosmos had a missing frequency. The frequency would establish a better communication between our cosmos and them. I found that out when I communicated with the Mother Goddess's unformed feminine aspects in one of the oceans of consciousness, which surrounds our cosmos. The unformed goddesses could not see, hear or assist very well—they seemed to have been in isolation within the surrounding layers of the cosmos.

I asked him if they were keepers of this frequency, he nodded "Yes." I asked whether they were waiting for the right time to restore it to the Mother for placement around the cosmos and he nodded "Yes." Then he was gone. I wondered why I had been left with the impression that he was sad.

In the early morning hours of the 18th of May, 2007 I saw, not in my room, but on the screen of my mind, another little man. He was vivid enough to wake me out of sleep. He was peeking very fearfully from

172

behind a half open door. The mouth was distorted into a grimace; the teeth were pointed.

His big dark eyes were full of fear. Like the other Stiblhaspava, his face was very wrinkled. He left me with an uneasy feeling. There should be joy at their return. Why did he give me the feeling of distortion?

Later that day, I received their glyphs with their translation and not long after, Mother gave the following information:

There were 867 of them who had entered the moon to safeguard the eighth frequency. This was done when the planet was twenty-two levels above where the cycles of the Great Fall had begun[84].

They had an energy source that could sustain them and none perished from lack.

A little more than two thirds doubted themselves and their abilities to fulfill their task. Their self-doubt also brought lack of trust in Mother. They could not leave the moon without going through the Mother's Blood (now surrounding every being and planetary body[85]) which meant they would cease to exist.

During May 18, 2007, the ones who had kept the faith, left the moon for Earth and restored the frequencies to Mother. They rejoiced at the completion of their task and confinement. But they were saddened by the loss of so many of their race. The restored frequency had to be purified by Mother, as it had picked up some of the doubt.

---

84. Described in *The Gift of the Unicorns*.
85. See the later section on the Additional Bodies of Man.

Communication from the Stiblhaspava

1. *Er varn hak eklas brin, stubal brunim brr vaarunim, Stiblhaspava eefrim prr klispiriha partunem.*

When the planet fell and light dimmed, the Stiblhaspava placed the frequency they held in the hollow moon, twenty-two levels above the cycles of the Great Fall.

2. *Gri brista bilisik brunem usprkl veesh. Tre uneem spereratvl. Erek natra utrinimi varanak.*

The Radiant Mother asked that the frequency of the eighth direction be safeguarded. This gave the eighth direction the qualities of a void. The realms (levels of existence) received insulation.

3. *Bareesh nen heraveet ska u lech bi-eesh ustivineem parkl uste vitl a ubleesh nau na u na veet ste-e-lah.*

Many times the six dark gods tried to enter the hollow moon, but (they) were unsuccessful.

4. *Stalak nutl veesh berespi austa. Branum Stillhaspava gri brista bilisik parveshpi u-alla uveesh stekl uspa ger stuvahet oblaveesh pa ukret stravaah.*

We kept the frequency safe. The Stiblhaspava return, the Radiant Mother requested that we restore the frequency to the void (to light up the void).

(Figure 58)

The Nitzkabelavek

April 19, 2007

Before the Nitzkabelavek actually arrived and were still approaching the cosmos, they appeared telepathically to two goddesses on Earth. One of the goddesses saw their faces and drew them for me. I recognized their race. During the construction of the wheels in 2005[86], they had appeared to me in a dream to give me their symbols for a specifc wheel, or cosmic gate.

The second goddess saw the leader of the Nitzkabelavek riding in a small coach. The leader wore a turban-like headpiece to indicate his status. The goddess saw only his head and shoulders through the coach window as he looked at her. His wife, not clearly seen, was in the background tending their baby. He came to give me his gifts the following night.

The Nitzkabelavek are between two and two-and-a-half feet in height and either go naked or wear very few clothes. When they do wear clothes, they mostly consist of just one piece; a pair of pants, for example. The only clothes I saw were made of feathers. They live in hollowed-out areas under trees. During the week the fairies permitted me into their world for the writing of *Arubafirina—The Book of Fairy Magic*, I had seen the inside of many of their homes. They had primitive but detailed furniture with many useful household items not dissimilar to some of ours. The Nitzkabelavek's homes have the barest minimum. Their 'bed' may be a piece of hollow bark covered with moss and feathers. Not much trouble is taken to produce furniture.

Their little bodies are rounded like those of toddlers and the impression of their being 'childlike' is enhanced by their round, hairless heads. Their faces have an owlish appearance because of the large eyes and pronounced brow ridges that become long, narrow, beak-

86. These wheels, constructed under the direction of the Mother Goddess and described in *Secrets of the Hidden Realms*, were designed to open interdimensional membranes during the Earth's ascension.

175

like noses. Their mouths are very small.

The gift they brought was knowledge, and although they 'downloaded' knowledge into me the next night (as with the other two kingdoms, their gifts are for everyone), I am not yet aware of what it is. They said exactly what the Arcturan fairies had said, namely that although it is downloaded, it would only be accessed when the time was right. These little beings' gift of coded subtle information was placed in the life force center and in the DNA.

The Darklings said that all of the Nitzkabelavek who were hidden, have returned and that there are between 1,500-2,000 of them. They are able to teleport themselves wherever they wish to go within moments—a special gift of this kingdom.

The Bekbavarabishpi—The Tree People
April 18, 2007

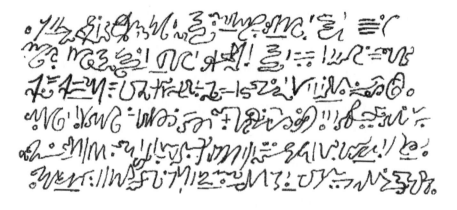

The Song of the Tree People
Baleesh veem uplahar veesh mee
Kle staa vaa usbees pla u nee
Stu baa u daa seesh vee uanee
Klee eshvee baa uf vra bee
Fraa hes baa ufraa bee una eesh
Kliaas brees virineesh tuaa vane

176

Our song like a wind in the trees
Bring glad tidings and good news
Of a time of great light that's begun
When the clans of truth once more return
Ancient secrets again revealed
Restoring joy to everyone's heart

Chorus:
Veesh treeush na neesh
Veesh treeush na neesh

Hear the voices in the wind
Hear the voices in the wind

I saw the Bekbavarabishpi clearly, and recognized them immediately from their artwork that had been part of the intricate, and sometimes large wheels[87] I was told by Mother to construct as tools to open the membranes between the realms as the Earth started to ascend in February 2005. As we have seen in *The Gift of the Unicorns*, during some of the cycles within the Fall, the Earth had either torn or bounced off a membrane when a gateway had not been created for her passage. The wheels, or gateways, and the kingdoms' contributions to their construction, were therefore essential to the Earth's ascension.

The Bekbavarabishpi originated in ancient Lemuria (called Shalmali at the time). They were hidden by Mother fourteen cycles of life ago and forsook living among the rest of the population in favor of living among the trees in heavily forested areas. They became known as the Tree People.

They had, and still have, the ability to materialize and de-materialize at will, sometimes entering into trees to hide. I asked why they had withdrawn from society. The answer was, "The trees are kinder."

There are 986 of them that returned to Earth on the date given above. I asked if, like the Ellamakusanek, any portion of them had lost faith and been unable to return into the cosmos. The answer came very quickly: "All love Mother. All here."

87. See Part I, *Secrets of the Hidden Realms*.

They live in caves or stone houses. I asked whether their stone houses were round or square like ours; "Round only when a cave." They are vegetarians. Their clothes are made from tree bark, but look more pliable and thinner than the bark 'cloth' called tapa, made by South Sea Islanders.

Physically their appearance is the epitome of refinement. Their build and features are delicate and well-formed. They have very light, almost white, blond hair and gentle, pale blue eyes. The adults stand between 20-22 feet tall. The initial contact with them was with a family of four: parents, an older daughter and younger son.

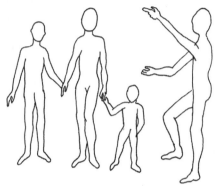

I was told they were very much hunted after Mother hid them because of the gifts they carried that pertain to sight. "You mean the ability to see realms above the one we're in?", I asked. "There are more ways to 'see' than that!" I asked for an example. "To see underneath what is happening." I asked whether they meant to see behind the appearances. "No, what's going on underneath." I did not quite understand, but did not press them further.

Their gifts are given by activating certain parts of the brain, as I later found out after an acute headache. I got the impression something was also done to the etheric lenses in the front and behind the eyes. My eyes were swollen and bloodshot after their work on me, which took place two nights after the initial contact. Like the other kingdoms, they were preparing us for evolution to super-humanness and their gifts were for everyone.

As in the case of the Ellamakusanek, an Earthly goddess was sent to bring them out of the void into our cosmos. She described to me the pocket of space (left behind in the void which is now purple[88]) in which they were waiting for Mother to send for them.

The rectangular pocket the Ellamakusanek were in was such a dark

88. See *The Ring of Truth* for the reason the void changed from black to purple.

indigo as to appear almost navy blue. The Bekbavarabishpi's pocket of space, however, was kite-shaped and the color of the throat chakra. The darker sky blue became lighter as she brought them closer to the cosmos. At all times during our interactions with them, they emanated a deep and gentle love.

Transmission from the Butterfly Fairies of the Eighth Body of our Cosmos

(Received by Master Barbara R.)

We are the Eeshvabruk. A group of us descended as part of the fairy realms into the lower realms when the Earth descended.

We descended voluntarily to help the Mother in Her days of sadness when She was alone. We bring lightness of heart with our presence.

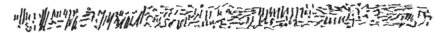

The stress of the density was too much for those of us who had descended and they perished and were no longer found during the last cycle of the Great Fall.

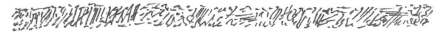

Now Earth and Mother have ascended once again to the levels of the Eeshvabruk and we have been asked to bring lightness of heart yet again.

We live in balls of light that change colors when we have different emotions. We have antennae on our heads and beautiful wings.

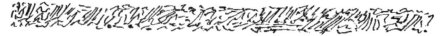

We are happiest when we are outside near flowers, but we hover around people to make their hearts happy.

Transmission from the Elves of the Eighth Body of the Cosmos
(Received by Master Barbara R.)

Birnm feeleesh parvim ustafrim spa-uruveet staarhem Kirtl usbaavrim hiri frim pa urtl barashvee.

We are the elves that stayed behind and supported those of us who left with the Mother in Her journey below.

Belesh brakvi kirtl hus navareem belesvaarnm esva uklesvi staa ureem parava.

We speak to the one who hears (they first contacted the master Barbara in one of my classes) because we do not want to be forgotten.

Vaarik frim bilavce-ares paarnm klee viravimpa ulaespi vifaleem rustavabi uskla ubravee.

We bring play and fun and laughter back to heal the wounds of the past. It is time for revelry to start.

Our Loop of Existence Within the Fall

Descension

Ascension

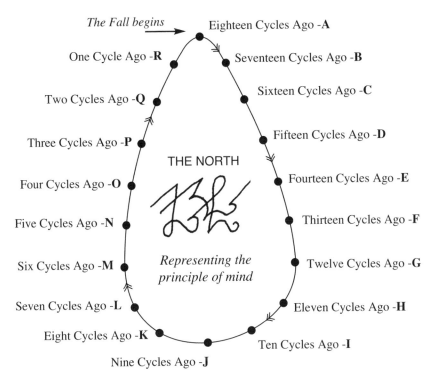

The Fall begins → Eighteen Cycles Ago -**A**

One Cycle Ago -**R**

Seventeen Cycles Ago -**B**

Two Cycles Ago -**Q**

Sixteen Cycles Ago -**C**

Three Cycles Ago -**P**

Fifteen Cycles Ago -**D**

THE NORTH

Four Cycles Ago -**O**

Fourteen Cycles Ago -**E**

Five Cycles Ago -**N**

Thirteen Cycles Ago -**F**

Representing the principle of mind

Six Cycles Ago -**M**

Twelve Cycles Ago -**G**

Seven Cycles Ago -**L**

Eleven Cycles Ago -**H**

Eight Cycles Ago -**K**

Ten Cycles Ago -**I**

Nine Cycles Ago -**J**

A – Britbranukheresva

B – Virshstranabirtnechparvu

C – Peleshnuastraparvet

D – Krugnavilnavek

E – Virshstaruchvi-ulesvavi

F – Michpresbarutkvechsbiubararut

G – Blavachseshiviherestag

H – Brimiheshvikluvasta

I – Stuavechkresvauvraverete

J – Stelemirkrunesviheresta

K – Verlachbravaheshpistrana-doch

L – Silviskratnutpeleshnutvi

M – Stravukletnutheresva

N – Blishblanucherestraunet

O – Stretbichbeleshvahufspavi

P – Mirvanadochstra-uvabach

Q – Kluvarechshpi-urvavech

R – Elvishvraklarespi

The nine descension cycles were called:
Klubatruaneshprispretvauklesbi

The nine ascension cycles were called:
Hurplesplek-urnavestresh-abruhelesvi-kluavachvra-kreunit

(Figure 59)

181

Transmission from the Dwarfs of the Eighth Cosmic Body

(Received by Master Barbara R.)

We are the dwarfs and we have been waiting for you to get here. We want to ask you something.

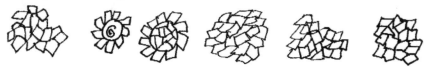

We have made new gemstones for the Earth[89]. There are five new ones but Mother must put the fire in them. Please, is it time? They are ready.

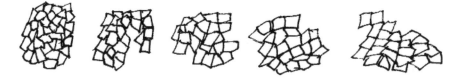

We have another gift for the Mother. It is a song. We will sing it to Her, please, to welcome Her back.

It is a song that must be sung over and over five times in your pretend dawn.

Note: it is an illusion that the sun rises and sets when it does—Mother kept this illusion in place since 2005 when the Earth ascended out of its former position in space.

---

89. To embody the five additional rays of light available to the Earth at this time.

Transmission from a Group of Giants Newly Arrived In the Inner Earth from the Nineth Cosmic Body

(Received by Master Barbara R.)

To the Mother praise. Our love and loyalty is pledged to Her forever. To be loved by a Giant is to feel great love.

Our children tell the tales of Her greatness. Her face is before us and Her words ring in our ears like music.

Transmission from the Highest Levels of Angels in our Cosmos[90] From the Ninth Cosmic Body

The heavens ring with our choruses of love
Long have we waited in realms above
For the light finally victorious to be
Our choruses raise in praise to Your victory
After eons of separation home You've come
Our hearts rejoice at our reunion

---

90. As of June 6, 2007. They gave their language to the Master Barbara R. during one of Almine's classes in May 2007.

Changing to Our Next Level of Evolution

In May 2007 Mother declared in the Book of Life (in which the laws of existence are written) that growth no longer comes from imbalance but from support. The old way, of the mental fields spinning 34 times counter-clockwise for every 21 times the magnetic, emotional fields spin clockwise, was changed. All life now had them spinning at equal speeds. (For a description of these fields, see the previous section on how all beings received a feeling body.)

She then moved every being's life force center (in humans a ball of white light about the size of a grapefruit) from behind the belly button to the heart center. This changed life from being logic-driven to love-driven. This is also the position of the life force center in some starbeings who are more conscious than humans. This began implementation of Her plan to give humankind an evolutionary boost.

During the same month, more interdependence rather than dependence was created in Her relationship with all beings. Two new forms of awareness were introduced into the cosmos—one feminine and one neutral in relation to our previous form. Her children can actually produce awareness, becoming co-creators in this way and by creating through the heart. They can do this by living the twelve pairs of pure emotions and twelve pure states of being (see Bonus Chapter). They can also pull awareness in from the sea of consciousness (the Infinite) outside the membrane containing our cosmos. In this way they can enhance cosmic awareness, adopting a more responsible and mature role as Her children.

- An etheric or energetic 'door' was opened in the pineal to receive awareness from the Infinite. The activation of the god-cell, a specific cell in the pineal gland, allows for the capacity to interpret this information. An etheric door was also opened in the heart to produce awareness by living the pure emotions and states of being.
- Some on Earth will begin to think simultaneously with surface mind, higher mind and fully expanded, highest mind. This will enable them to keep the large blueprint or plan in mind, while seeing behind the appearances, but also attending to the details. *(Fig. 60, The Nine Bodies of Man)*

The Nine Bodies of Man

(Corresponding with the Nine Bodies of the Cosmos)

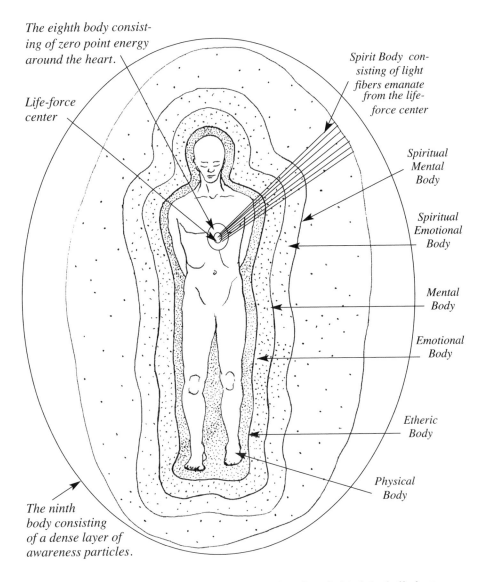

The eighth body consisting of zero point energy around the heart.

Life-force center

Spirit Body consisting of light fibers emanate from the life-force center

Spiritual Mental Body

Spiritual Emotional Body

Mental Body

Emotional Body

Etheric Body

Physical Body

The ninth body consisting of a dense layer of awareness particles.

In April 2007, man's life force center was moved up from behind the belly button to the heart center. In May 2007, the cosmos, and man as the microcosm, received the eighth and ninth bodies. The eighth body consists of zero point energy around the heart chakra (now surrounded also by the small sphere of life force).

(Figure 60)

185

The Additional Bodies of Man

On May 17, 2007, the Mother Goddess gave a part of Herself to all creatures and beings (such as planetary bodies). She created a dense layer of Her light to surround every living being, and around that She placed a layer of a substance that is the equivalent to the Infinite's blood—we shall call it Mother's Blood.

The purpose of this is as a form of insulation. After eons of outside tampering, Mother has devised a way of insulating each being. No invasion from any hostile beings can penetrate Mother's Blood. It is the substance She uses to safeguard the cosmos itself during this and the previous cycle of life.

Mother's Blood can be called 'physical' in that it is from Her densest, or most physical part. In physicality opposites repel, however, as explained in the Belvaspata section later in this book. All beings protected only with this 'blood' would therefore have felt repelled by Mother's Blood. This would eventually have caused a repelling of Mother Herself, since Her physicality is different from that of Her creations.

The laws of existence also decree that opposite light attracts. Mother has therefore placed a dense level of Her light within the shield of blood. This will bring several advantages to every being:

• Her creations will feel attraction versus a repelling of Mother. If we study the history of the cycles (see The History of the Cycles in *The Gift of the Unicorns*), we will find that this brings ascension rather than descension.

• It will form a further shield to prevent even more subtle forms of invasion from reaching the individual being.

• The Belvaspata healing modality is highly effective because of opposite light attracting. Having Mother's greater light around us, is like having permanent healing taking place. The perfect light is attracted to any distorted light and can be attracted out of its layer to the site of distortion. Healing will take place if we do not hold on to the illusion of the disease.

Call for Purification of Illusion Through the Tenth Body

*Barisk tretva uhurus tre tra va
Tru-u spa u ratvi ek stanadok
Berespa. Nin kretvi erestra uesbi
Kletl hut spa-u rak viles taa.*

Cleanse from my body every trace
Of aught that of negativity remains.
By the Mother's Blood's power, let it be so
I release all resistance, only light shall I know.

Understanding the Bodies of Man

Just like all other parts of dynamic life, the bodies of man (and all beings) pulse between receptive and pro-active, between allowing input and giving output.

The two lowest bodies of man (the etheric and the physical) express the being's individuality and potential. The two higher bodies (emotional and mental) are designed to receive the highest wisdom from the three highest bodies. When the mental body tries to run one's life, the upper guidance (including the healing influence of Mother's light) cannot penetrate and be passed on to the physical for expression.

The three highest bodies of spiritual emotional, spiritual mental and the spirit body function as follows: *(See Fig. 61, Additional Bodies Given: Living in Mother's Light)*

- The potential of the cosmos lies within the light fibers of man but it lies in a dormant state until it 'lights up'—like being brought online.
- The zero point body around the heart helps us to create our realities through love.
- The awareness body receives ever-changing potential from the layer of Mother's Light around the fields for the heart to interpret and create as a reality.
- This is then passed on to the light fibers in the spirit body which light up certain of these light fibers so that new perception can take place. *(See Fig. 62, The Autonomy of the Bodies of Man)*

187

Additional Bodies Given: Living in Mother's Light

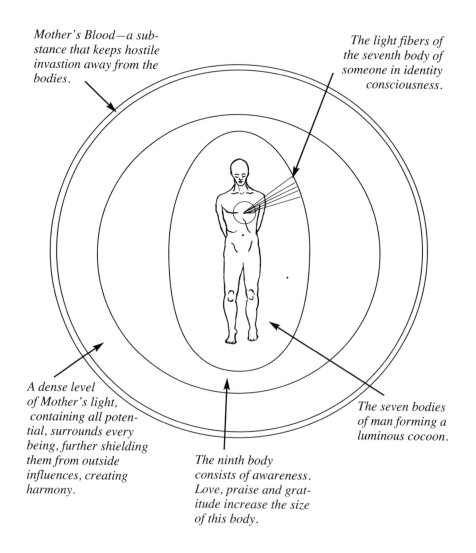

Mother's Blood—a substance that keeps hostile invastion away from the bodies.

The light fibers of the seventh body of someone in identity consciousness.

A dense level of Mother's light, containing all potential, surrounds every being, further shielding them from outside influences, creating harmony.

The ninth body consists of awareness. Love, praise and gratitude increase the size of this body.

The seven bodies of man forming a luminous cocoon.

(Figure 61)

The Autonomy of the Bodies of Man

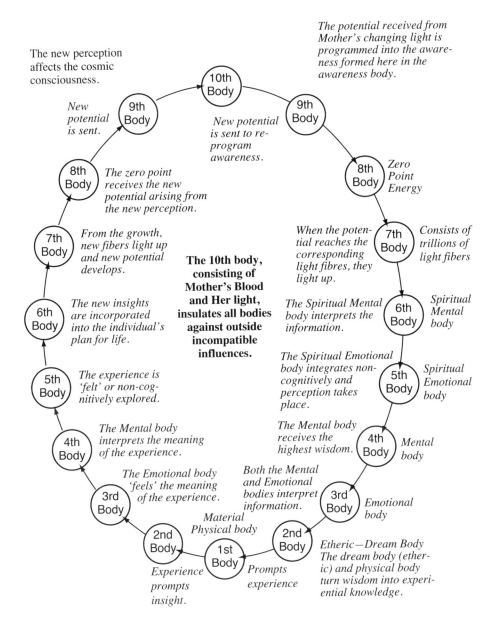

The new perception affects the cosmic consciousness.

New potential is sent.

The potential received from Mother's changing light is programmed into the awareness formed here in the awareness body.

New potential is sent to re-program awareness.

The zero point receives the new potential arising from the new perception.

10th Body

9th Body

9th Body

8th Body

Zero Point Energy

7th Body

From the growth, new fibers light up and new potential develops.

The 10th body, consisting of Mother's Blood and Her light, insulates all bodies against outside incompatible influences.

When the potential reaches the corresponding light fibres, they light up.

Consists of trillions of light fibers

6th Body

The new insights are incorporated into the individual's plan for life.

The Spiritual Mental body interprets the information.

Spiritual Mental body

5th Body

The experience is 'felt' or non-cognitively explored.

The Spiritual Emotional body integrates non-cognitively and perception takes place.

Spiritual Emotional body

4th Body

The Mental body interprets the meaning of the experience.

The Mental body receives the highest wisdom.

Mental body

3rd Body

The Emotional body 'feels' the meaning of the experience.

Both the Mental and Emotional bodies interpret information.

Emotional body

2nd Body

Material Physical body

1st Body

2nd Body

Etheric—Dream Body The dream body (etheric) and physical body turn wisdom into experiential knowledge.

Experience prompts insight.

Prompts experience

The flow of information occurs in a self-directing and autonomous manner.
Potential is ever-increasing through the contribution of experience.

(Figure 62)

189

Closing

The great privilege of being the scribe of a body of most holy scriptures cannot be expressed in words. The body of information is vast enough that, in fact, a whole series of books can be written from it.

It is the first time that information for two books was given at once. Even as *The Gift of the Unicorns* was being received, information from the Isis mysteries was also made available. Though I found the in-pouring of two streams of information very challenging at first, over time I began understanding the reason for this strange turn of events.

First, the cosmic history revealed by the race known as the Darklings for the Unicorn book was dovetailing beautifully with the Isis material. It would present a much fuller picture if read together. Receiving them together enabled me to better choose which portions of the vast body of Isis material to transcribe for this book.

It may present the question that if portions of the Unicorn book meshed so well with this one, why they were not placed into one volume. Over the years of writing these books, it has become clear that the timing and content of these books are pre-determined. At times books have had to be written at breakneck speed in order to fall within a set time for releasing the information to the world.

An example of how information is earmarked for a certain book can be explained as follows: The Darklings had wanted to give us their body of magic. They specifically requested that it be part of this book, even though they had made such a major contribution to the Unicorn book. They explained that their magic's frequency would be more compatible with this one. But Mother's information filled the pages instead.

I suggested we create a book for their magic and that of the dragons. This suggestion was met with a stunned silence at first, then they patiently explained that that was impossible; the frequencies were too different. I then asked whether the large body of magic the Arcturian fairies wanted to convey would work side-by-side with theirs (even though the Arcturian fairies had requested their own book!) but again, the frequencies were not compatible.

The sacred languages given in this book, convey non-cognitive information to the right brain even as the words inform the left brain. The many reasons why the words are presented in verse, are not yet fully clear to me. It is apparent though, that it reminds the reader not to take the words at face value, but rather to feel the information with one's heart. Rereading it with the humility of not thinking we know, will reveal multiple levels of information.

The Riddle to Change All Life, given by the Mother, provides us a challenge and as always, it is someone in human form who has to turn the key. Which of us will be the first to unravel the mysteries held in its words, to find the new way of changing the dream? It is in the physical where all new information is gained. It is therefore only here where the key can be turned to usher in a new luminous way of life.

My deep love and respect to my light family here on Earth, and to Mother the glory forever and ever.

Into Grand Mastery With Belvaspata

Belvaspata: From Initiate to Grand Mastery Level
Preparations Required for Each Level and for Self-initiations

Level I connects the initiate to the soul group they represent.

    Study and internalize the 12 Pairs of Emotions

    Self-initiation for Level I

    (Can heal with the sigils of Love.)[91]

Level II connects the initiate to the planetary grid. Each time a Level II practitioner uses Belvaspata, it affects all humanity through his/her connection to the grid.

    Study and internalize the 16 Rays of Light

    Self-initiation for Level II

    (Can heal with the sigils of Love and the sigils of Light.)

Master Level removes illusion, connecting the Master to the cosmic grid.

    Study and internalize the 12 Pure Pairs of States of Being

    Self-initiation for Master Level

    (Can initiate others up to Mastery level and heal with sigils of Love, Light and States of Being.)

Grand Master Level affects the spiritual emotional, spiritual mental and spirit bodies of all. It is the level to prepare for immortality of the body, as it releases new hormones and opens higher capacities of

---

91. Initiation sigils can be used by those practicing Belvaspata at this level in healing others. Only Masters and Grand Masters can initiate practitioners up to and including their own level.

the endocrine system. It also clears the cosmic pathways and removes old programming of suffering as it connects the initiate with assistance from the highest levels within the cosmos.

Study and internalize the 12 Pairs of Heart Energies

Self-initiation for Grand Mastery Level

(Can use all sigils of Grand Mastery and below and initiate others up to Grand Mastery)

Introduction

Belvaspata, healing of the heart, is a sacred modality that heals with light and frequency. This healing method is a gift from the creator Goddess to the cosmic races to accommodate the changing laws of physics that took place as all life ascended into a new creation in August 2006. The use of Belvaspata heals the environment as the sacred sigils connect the practitioner to the planetary grids. *(See Fig. 63, The Sigil for Belvaspata)*

Belvaspata, the Healing Modality

Belvaspata, the healing modality for the new frequencies within the cosmos, takes into consideration changes that occurred in August 2006, altering the laws governing all existence.

The most basic assumptions on which healers of all modalities have based their methods, changed overnight. In the past, opposite energies attracted and healing energy gravitated towards diseased energies. Now, they reject each other. Instead, healers can now utilize light and frequency to dispel the illusion of disease, since under the changed cosmic laws, their opposite aspects attract.

Belvaspata, in the language of the Mother Goddess, means 'healing of the heart'. Whereas the primary purpose of previous cycles of existence was to seek perception (which is mind-oriented), the one we have entered has a different purpose. This creation challenges us to fulfill one primary purpose: **To create through the heart.**

The body of knowledge which is Belvaspata, is a gift from the Mother that we may fulfill the new purpose of life. It is here to help us

The Sigil for Belvaspata

Belvaspata
Healing of the Heart

The Over-all Angel for Belvaspata

Kelechnutvaveleshvispata
Angel sigil:

(Figure 63)

The Twelve Bands of Emotion of the Cosmos

In the previous cycle light formed the matrix of the cosmos, while emotion and awareness moved. In the new cycle, rings of emotion form the matrix. Omnipresent awareness permeates everything.

The bands are represented by 12 Goddesses. Each band represents two opposite poles of emotion. The poles pulse each other.

(Figure 64)

create health, joy and happiness through the heart.

Integrating the Twelve Frequencies

In preparation for Belvaspata's Level I initiation, the initiate must integrate the twelve frequencies (emotions) that comprise the twelve frequency bands of the cosmos. At least one whole day should be put aside for this. Once initiated, the practitioner may heal using these frequencies and their sigils. *(See Fig. 64, The Twelve Bands of Emotion)*

The Emotions

Each pair of emotions represents a ring and its masculine and feminine aspects. They pulse against each other to enhance the qualities of both. The stronger one feels a specific emotion, the deeper one can go into its opposite aspect. In fact, the more strongly an emotion is felt, the more its opposite must be experienced or an overbalance results. For instance, if one does not alternate achievement with fun, it can become blind ambition, losing sight of the quality of the journey.

It is essential that the steps be performed in the same order as the frequencies are found in their spheres within the cosmos, starting from the core emotions of love and trust, and working your way out to growth and satisfaction.

To internalize an emotion, we approach it from the largest perspective:

- While in a meditative state, visualize your heart center opening wider and wider until you can imagine seeing the whole Earth in it;
- Imagine and visualize the heart center opening at a rate beyond the speed of light until the solar system, the galaxy and then many galaxies are visible through the heart;
- Continue opening while in deep meditation until the whole cosmos is within you and you have reached the membrane that contains it all;
- The large central sun will now be within you and you will see its arms of light spiraling outwards, consisting of trillions upon trillions of galaxies like specks of light;
- Remind yourself that you are a consciousness superimposed over all that is and you are all that you see;

- From this large perspective, feel the frequency of the emotion ripple through you as you envision all that evokes it;
- Sustain it until it is strong, potent and all you can feel;
- When you've become the emotion, understand and observe how it pulses with its opposite aspect;
- When you can feel them both, move on to the next emotion while keeping the expanded awareness;
- Each pair of emotions should be explored and experienced for about half an hour.

The Twelve Pairs of Emotions

Positive Aspect   *Negative Aspect*

1. Love   **Trust**
The desire to include   The desire to surrender
                             (replaces fear)

2. Inspiration   **Peace**
The desire to be inspired   The desire to be at ease
and to inspire (replaces anger) (replaces protectiveness)

3. Creativity   **Pleasure**
The desire to create   The desire to be delighted

4. Empathy   **Acknowledgement**
The desire to connect   The desire to see the perfection

5. Generosity   **Receptivity**
The desire to give   The desire to receive

6. Encouragement   **Beauty**
The desire to encourage   The desire to be uplifted
or to be encouraged

7. Communication   **Assimilation**
The desire to express   The desire to integrate

8. Passion
    The desire to know

Joy
    The desire to live

9. Achievement
    The desire to excel

Fun
    The desire to revel

10. Enlightenment
    The desire to enhance or
    be enhanced (replaces pain)

Contentment
    The desire to retain

11. Empowerment
    The desire to be of service

Humor
    The desire to be amused

12. Growth
    The desire to expand

Satisfaction
    The desire to be fulfilled

1. Trust and Love

Trust and Love are the core emotions for the new creation of existence and replace fear.

As old programming of fear breaks down in every being, the new reality of trust must reveal itself. It is, after all, what is real; what **is**. All else is just an illusion.

Trusting that our lives are guided in every way by our largest identity that spans all existence, we can release our attempts to control life. But what guides our highest self? The One Life that sustains us all—infinite, timeless and vast.

In your expanded state, feel the essence of the One Infinite Being, the serenity, compassion and ageless wisdom. Feel your expanded being as part of this Infinite's vastness and all-encompassing love. This is what runs all life. Allow yourself to surrender to the guidance and love of the Infinite.

The more we surrender to the One, to ourselves, the deeper our love for all beings grows. We can include them in our love because we see so clearly that the roles we play in our experiences are but small ones on a small stage. When we look further, each being is a unique perspective superimposed over all that is—just as vast as we are and just as deserving of life as a part of the Infinite's Being.

Allow love, trust and total surrender to flood your being until they have become part of all you are.

2. Peace and Inspiration

Peace and Inspiration form the second ring. Peace is the desire to be at home, to feel totally at ease. These rings build on each other; we cannot feel peace when trust is not present, telling us that life is safe. Peace knows that the cosmos is a safe home; that we can relax in the knowledge that we are in the secure hands of our highest self.

The striving that was part of linear progression in the previous cycle, left us feeling we always had to become what we were not. The new creation offers us an unprecedented gift that makes striving unnecessary. All is available right now in terms of awareness. All we have to do is open the door in each moment using the ascension attitudes.[92] These attitudes come when we cease to strive and are fully at ease within the moment.

This deep peace creates our happiness and acceptance of our body as the center of our cosmic home. This is not something light workers have generally felt. Many have been unaccustomed to dense bodies, having been seeded into humanity as a gift of light during the earth's pivotal role during the cosmic ascension.

They've wanted to leave their bodies, at times even living partially out of body. Where is there to go if we are everywhere at once? We are neither the body nor its experiences. Secure in this knowledge, we can be at peace and enjoy the play.

This feeling of being at peace within ourselves and at home in the cosmos, did not come easily in the previous cycle for another very prominent reason. Since opposites attracted, we were surrounded by opposite energy. The greater our light, the greater the darkness that lurked behind the faces we drew into our environment.

Now that the same energies attract each other, we will be attracting others who live the same high standards of impeccability. We will finally not only feel at home within ourselves but also with others. We must be able to allow those with opposite energies to depart with grace, however, for in keeping with the new laws of the cosmos, their departure is

92. See Appendix IV.

inevitable. It is also inevitable that others with like energies must gravitate towards us.

It is in the deep peace of our being that we access the perfection of all life. It is here inspiration is born. We are now immortal in our individuated beings, and physical immortality is available also through constant states of the ascension attitudes. We have now every reason to be inspired, to build a life of beauty and a legacy that inspires others.

3. Creativity and Pleasure

The link between Creativity and Pleasure is apparent, as the more pleasure fills our life, the more the muse stirs us into creativity. The more creative we become, the more our pleasure increases.

This pair of emotions, together with the previous two rings, forms the core of the new creation. That such pleasant and worthy emotions have replaced anger, pain, fear and protectiveness is a cause for gratitude and great praise. They form the hub, or core of the rings of frequency, inspiring creativity through love—the primary purpose for life.

To be constantly delighted simply takes full awareness of the moment. When we truly experience the wonder of the senses, the beauty of Creation all around us and the heroism that lies in everyday life, delight will flood our being. Only those unaware, or steeped in thought, can deprive themselves of the pleasure life so freely offers the one who lives in the moment.

4. Acknowledgement and Empathy

See the ever-unfolding perfection underlying appearances. It is not enough to acknowledge that the perfection is there, then feel victimized by someone a while later. Do we truly realize that we have co-created whatever is in our life?

If we do not like what we have created, it is now easier for us to make changes since the very purpose of this new paradigm is creating through love. If we focus on that which we love, new creation will flow. If we focus on that which we do not like, the change will not come. In this new creation, therefore, we have come into our spiritual maturity; we have become co-creators with the Infinite. The perfection is not just there for us to **find**; it is ours to create.

How do we create perfection? We create it by finding it in others, in the moment, in the situation. We create that which we love in another. Light workers no longer need to be surrounded by those of an opposite energy. It should therefore be easy to see perfection in those we draw into our lives.

When we focus on perfection, our ability to find it increases. Our life will be increasingly filled by a light family. In the safety of being among others like us, we empathically connect. The opposite aspect of acknowledgement is the desire to connect—empathy.

Encounters with those of lower light also allow a heart connection because, in seeing their perfection, we connect with the perfection of their higher selves, not their lowest. In seeing this, we help them to achieve that perfection. But it does not mean we have to allow them into our lives.

Now, it is safe for us to connect empathically with others. We are no longer the martyrs. We no longer have to be injured so others may learn. Because our hearts are open, we have become cosmic creators. This is a role so precious and significant that we cannot allow any remaining illusion in another to close off this priceless connection we have with all life—the gift of empathy.

5. Receptivity and Generosity

When a large cycle closes, as has just occurred, not only do opposite poles reverse but, as a consequence, their flow is also reversed. In the previous cycle, light workers were surrounded by those who wanted their light. The takers were not consciously aware of what they were seeking, so they took anything they could get. Light workers, therefore, have been giving for ages while others have been taking.

Now the flow has reversed and the debt has to be paid. There is a law of compensation decreeing that imbalance in any part of existence must have an equal and opposite movement to correct it. This is about to happen as light workers are repaid for all their giving.

There is just one requirement, however, and that is receptivity. After only giving for so long, light workers must break the mindset that can stand in the way of opening to receive. They must, in fact, look forward to it, expect it and envision it.

There has been an agenda associated with others giving to us that has sometimes made us reluctant to receive. But if it is the cosmos settling a score, we are really getting what belongs to us by rights. What does it then matter through what means it chooses to repay us? Let us be filled with receptivity.

When we give, we must not think that such generosity depletes us. Rather let us see how generosity and receptivity form one long continuous flow. Though the wind blowing through the house enters at the window, it leaves through the door.

Express both receptivity and generosity joyously.

6. Beauty and Encouragement

It can be said that beauty is just a glimpse into the perfection of the indwelling life behind form. It sees that which has enduring value, like a doorway into eternity. Every time we recognize beauty, we are encouraged (encouragement being its opposite aspect).

Beauty encourages us to create our life as a living work of art. If we see ourselves surrounded by beauty, we are hallowed by it. Moments become meaningful. A hard journey through life becomes not only tolerable, but we feel encouraged enough to believe we can flourish rather than survive.

There are obvious visions of beauty: the sunset over the sea, a child's sleeping face, a new kitten. But the true disciple of beauty doesn't stop there. Encouraged by what has become a treasure hunt for gems of beauty, he seeks to find them in the most unlikely places.

Artists of old saw beauty in the mundane, in another man's trash. They painted the crumbs of a left over meal, the spill of a wineglass. For where others saw only dirty dishes, the artist saw light as it played on crystal and wine and reflected off a wayward spoon.

They did not paint objects, but a dance of light, playfully leading the eye of the observer across the canvas of a captured moment. A famous English watercolorist said at the end of his life that he had never seen anything ugly. These are the words of a true disciple of beauty.

7. Assimilation and Communication

Too little true assimilation of information (which is accessed light) takes place in the world for several reasons:

- True listening to another's words can only take place in the absence of internal dialog. The listener has to stay in the silence of the mind and enter into the other's viewpoint by feeling the communication with the heart.
- The past cycle was left-brain dominated, but the non-verbal communications from the right brain accesses nine times more than did the left brain. The subtle information from the cosmos around us got crowded out by thought.
- Finding silence is getting more and more difficult. Airplanes roar, car horns blare, appliances hum and then, as though that were not enough, TVs are on whether someone is watching or not. Cell phones make sure that no one has silent time around them. But it is in silence that we get to know ourselves through listening to our thoughts and desires.
- Conversation and intergenerational communication has dwindled in most cultures where TV has become the substitute for knowing one another.
- We spend too little time in appreciation of nature's wonders, and much of that experience has become action-oriented. All of the natural world and its creatures speak to us through their individual frequencies. We can assimilate their special life song by sitting in silence and feeling it within our cells.

The assimilation of other's communications enriches us. Their diversity can carve new facets in our own life, new perspectives that leave us enhanced. When we feel truly heard, the desire to communicate (its opposite aspect) becomes more active as well.

8. Passion and Joy

When the social conditioning of our lives has left the clear impression that it is unsafe to fully participate in the game of life, we may hang back in the safety of the known, afraid to make ourselves a target by being noticed. We may fear that passion could cause our light to shine so brightly that others might try and tear us down so that their own lack of luster is not as obvious.

If we deny our desire to express passionately long enough, we end up being strangers to passion; not knowing how to find it, nor recognize it even if we do. The lateral hypothalamus tells us when we have eaten enough. The ventromedial hypothalamus tells us when we are hungry. In the same way, if we deny the promptings from these portions of the brain, we will end up either obese or anorexic. When that happens we have to gently coach ourselves into recalling how their promptings feel.

When passion beckons, we feel warm and excited; our faces flush and our imagination stirs with questions of "What if?" and "What lies beyond the next horizon?" It inspires us into action and makes us believe we can take risks and build.

We find our passion by following the yearnings our moments of joy evoke within our hearts. It is the lost song the singer feels hiding within the shadows of his mind; the lost rhythm the dancer forever seeks; the mysteries of the cosmos that wait for the scientist or the metaphysician to unlock. It is the desire, inspired by the innocence in our child's eyes, to build a life of wonder and beauty for our family.

If passion has become a stranger to us, we may need to become reacquainted with it one facet at a time. When it is expressed, passion consists of taking risks. It is the precursor to accomplishment and the building of something new. It adds new experiences, further boundaries, and new depth to our lives.

To train ourselves to hear the voice of passion again, we find the yearning of our heart and follow where it leads. We make a concerted effort to break free from the prison bars of ruts and expectations, socially conditioned limitations and self-imposed belief systems that keep us in mediocrity. We take a few minutes a day to dare to dream of what would make our hearts sing. We awake each morning and determine to live the day before us as though it were our last. We look at our lives as though for the first time, with a fresh perspective that can detect the joyless, self-sacrificing areas. With courage and great consideration for the consequences of our actions on others, we implement our first steps to bring the glow of passion back to these areas.

A decision may take a minute to make, but for it to be as life-altering as we would want it to be, it must be supported by a firm foundation. This requires planning and a certain amount of analysis. What is the goal? What resources will be needed? Is there a discrepancy between what we need and what we have? How can we fill it? Many businesses fail, taking many dreams with them, because not enough thought was given to what was needed to support them in terms of time and money. Once a goal is identified, break it into projects and tasks.

Many envy the achievements of others, but are not prepared to put in the work. Sometimes it takes burning the candle on both ends to fulfill a dream. It is our passion that keeps our enthusiasm lit and gives us our second wind to fly higher than we ever thought possible.

As passion explores the multitude of possibilities through which we can express, so joy is concentrated on the simplicity of the moment. Joy is a mindset, a certain focus that sees the perfection of the here and now, casting a golden glow over the experiences of yesterday. It turns the mundane into poetry and captures the moment in a still-life image.

Milton said: "The mind in its own place and of itself can turn hell into heaven and heaven into hell." Franz Lizt was urged to write his memoirs, but he said: "It is enough to have lived such a life." He found such joy in his experiences, he did not have to externalize them to appreciate them.

Joy can be recognized by the deep feeling of satisfaction it brings; by the feeling that one has come home to oneself. It taps into the quiet place within that nurtures the soul and replenishes the mind. When we are under its spell, joy makes us feel light and young again, connected to the earth and freed from our cares.

Just as building with passion requires careful and disciplined time allocations, living with joy requires us to focus on the details in front of us at the moment. Even if we cannot find even a moment today to do the things we enjoy, we can find the time to enjoy the things we are doing. In cutting up vegetables to make a stew, we can see the colors of the carrots, explore the different textures of each vegetable, smell the fresh fragrance as we cut through their skins.

Even repetitive work can become a mantra, or a production line a prayer as we send blessings and angelic assistance to the homes where the products will end up. Walking in the crowded street, we can feel the sadness of others but can turn it into joy by envisioning blessings pouring into their lives. The loss in the lives of others can be used to inspire praise and gratitude for the blessings in our own.

In our choice of the joy to fill our leisure time, we look for that which will inspire us into accomplishment. As the joy flows inward on the surface, the passion it inspires folds outward beneath the surface. The greater our joy, the greater the actions it will inspire.

9. Fun and Achievement

We have possibly all heard the saying that someone we know "works hard and plays hard". That is because the two go hand-in-hand. Fun without achievement is a shallow, unfulfilling life. Achievement without the fun that brings quality to the journey, leads to an equally unsatisfying life. Blind ambition can result from such an imbalance and one becomes blinded as to which achievements would be truly life-enhancing.

Fun helps energy flow and prevents us from taking ourselves too seriously. It relieves the tensions we experience during our battles of achievement.

10. Contentment and Enlightenment

Contentment knows that it is living perfect moments; the fire is crackling in the fireplace, a little child with sleep-weighted eyelids is wrapped in a quilt on your lap, while the rain of a winter night beats outside on the window panes.

It is during those moments that we wish everyone on earth could share the feeling—complete contentment. We wish we could enhance the life of a runaway teenager somewhere in a lonely bus station. We want to have the hungry family in the ghetto fed and feeling the inner fulfillment contentment brings.

Such contentment can come as a strong undercurrent of life, rather than as a few fleeting moments. Contentment as a constant companion is the result of deep, meaningful living—of insights gained and inner storms weathered. The desire to enhance and enlighten the life of another is the sincere wish that insight will change despair into contentment for another as well.

11. Empowerment and Humor

Empowerment is the desire to serve. At first, this definition might not make sense. The connection between service and empowerment might seem a bit obscure. The reason is that man has really not understood the proper meaning of service.

Service has often meant assuaging our conscience by giving a handout, not really addressing the deficiency that caused the condition in the first place. True service instead is empowering the individual to find his own way out of the dire straits of his life. This way he has something to show for his hardship; new-found strength or abilities.

The desire to be of service will be never-ending if it is based on need. As Christ said, *"The poor will always be among us."* It could eventually pull us into the despair of need as well. The balancing factor is humor.

Humor laughs at life, laughs at self and, instead of blaming, laughs at the folly of others. It cannot take anything too seriously because it knows without a shadow of doubt that we are just engaged in a play. It helps by empowering the beggar, not because he seems needy, but just because it is his role. The play must go on because it has value.

12. Growth and Satisfaction

Understanding the essence of growth is new. This is because the way growth now takes place is new. It used to be the result of delving (painfully, at times) into the unknown, grappling with its illusion and eventually turning it into the known through experience. When delving into the unknown, fear resulted, often bringing about protectiveness. When the illusion refused to yield its insights, anger tried to break it up.

The emotions associated with growth were not always pleasant and even the word "growth" often had an unpleasant connotation. Growth is now an expansion that is the result of satisfaction.

When we are with those who are energetically incompatible, we experience a shrinking feeling. The new creation brings kindred spirits in the form of family and friends. In the deep satisfaction of their company, we can feel our souls expand.

Growth used to come through opposition. Now it comes through support. How will we know when we have found it? The deep satisfaction of our hearts will tell us we have just lived our highest truth.

Symbols vs. Sigils

To understand sigils, we must first understand what symbols entail. We will also need to know the meanings of sigils in order to properly understand and utilize them as they are given later in this book.

A symbol **represents** something, whereas a sigil **describes** something. When someone sees a BMW or a Mercedes symbol, it represents upper middle-class vehicles of quality and distinction. On the other hand, the symbol for a Rolls Royce or Bentley represents elite vehicles that speak of a privileged lifestyle of dignity and wealth.

So much is deduced just from one symbol. A Rolls Royce evokes images of walled estates, chauffeurs, enough and accustomed money as opposed to the symbol of a Ferrari which speaks of more flamboyant taste.

Whereas symbols are common in our everyday world, the use of sigils is virtually forgotten. Even in mystery schools, their hidden knowledge eludes most mystics. But throughout the cosmos all beings of expanded awareness utilize sigils and only a few left-brain oriented races use symbols and those primarily in alphabets. The reason is this:

If we use the word 'LOVE', we have combined four symbols (letters representing certain sounds) to make one symbol (the word that represents a feeling). But love is one of the building blocks of the cosmos, like space or energy[93]. It can also represent many different nuances within the emotion of love (which is the desire to include) and many other disfunctionality and degrees of need we mistakenly call 'love.'

As we can see, the symbol or word can be very misleading since what it represents to one may not be what it represents to another. The sigil for love describes the quality or frequency of what is meant. It maps out the exact frequency of the emotion.

The sigil for someone's name would do the same. As the person or being rises in frequency, the sigil will change to reflect that. In the case of angels, even their names change. That is why the angel names or the goddess names have changed as the cosmos and Earth have ascended to

---

93. Discussed in *Journey to the Heart of God*, p. 56, The True Nature of the Seven Directions.

a much higher frequency[94]. In these higher realms the languages are different and reflect the higher frequencies.

When a person has accomplished a major task within the cosmos pertaining to the agreement they made with the Infinite, they also receive a 'meaning' with its accompanying sigil. When a being is called to do a task meant for the highest good, that being will come if you have its name and meaning. The being absolutely must come if, in addition, you have the sigil for the name and meaning.

Having someone's sigil is like having that person's phone number. Sigils not only describe what they represent, but are a means to communicate with what they represent.

The Significance of the Sigils

If all other healing modalities are having their healing energy, and their symbols meant to produce healing energy repulsed, they are in fact producing the opposite of what is intended.

Because disease is distorted energy that repulses the natural healing energies (the trillions of little fragments of awareness that have been available to restore perfection), these methods would produce disease.

On August 17, 2006, in order to prevent well-intentioned healers from doing harm, the Mother Goddess took away the power behind healing modalities based on energy work. The power behind the previously used symbols was also removed. It is for this reason that the gift of Belvaspata was given to humanity.

The Significance of the Master Sigil

The master sigil is to be used only for initiations of master practitioners because of the following purpose held within its power:

The sigils of Belvaspata have a hidden power behind the obvious. Every time they are used, they dispel the illusion of disease and the illusion of distortions found everywhere in light and frequency. In other words, when these sigils are used there is less disease everywhere on

---

94. See higher goddess names in *Secrets of the Hidden Realms*

Initiation Sigils Level I
Belvaspata Healing Modality
(Healing of the Heart)
All 3 sigils are used to start all healing sessions.

1.

To be drawn 3 times over the forehead
Blautvapata
Opening of the **mind**

angel sigil:

Call in the angel: Rutsetvi-uru-bach
(look at the angel sigil while calling angel name)

2.

To be drawn 3 times over the heart
Kruvechpaururek
Opening of the **heart**

angel sigil:

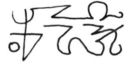

Call in the angel: Iornumubach
(look at the angel sigil while calling angel name)

3.

To be drawn 3 times over the navel
Kelavisbavah
Receptivity of the **body**

angel sigil:

Call in the angel: Tru-ararir-pleva
(look at the angel sigil while calling angel name)

(Figure 65)

Initiation Sigils Level II

(When healing, use in conjunction with Level I's sigils to start the session.)

1.

To be drawn 3 times over the lower abdomen
Kelavisvauravech
Release of patterns that no longer serve (transformation)

angel sigil:

Call in the angel: Krunechva-atruha
(look at the angel sigil while calling angel name)

2.

To be drawn 3 times over the solar plexus
Trechsubareshvi
Transmuting matter to higher light

angel sigil:

Call in the angel: Mirakluvael
(look at the angel sigil while calling angel name)

3.

To be drawn 3 times over the sternum
Patauruhutvi
Transfiguring illusion to light

angel sigil:

Call in the angel: Kelevi-traunar
(look at the angel sigil while calling angel name)

(Figure 66)

4.

To be drawn 3 times over the crown
Kersbaurveshpi
Sanctification

angel sigil:

Call in the angel: Trechbar-uru-heresvi
(look at the angel sigil while calling angel name)

5.

To be drawn 3 times over the throat
Kletsutmanarech
Attracting light into the voice

angel sigil:

Call in the angel: Vilivesbi-keres-na
(look at the angel sigil while calling angel name)

6.

*To be drawn 3 times over
each hand*
Visbelespahrechvi
Attracting healing frequencies
into the hands

angel sigil:

Call in the angel: Kru-echna-vilshpreva
(look at the angel sigil while calling angel name)

(Figure 67)

7.

To be drawn 3 times over the root chakra
Nenhershbikletrasut
DNA activation of the codes of light

angel sigil:

Call in the angel: Ku-ulu-vet
(look at the angel sigil while calling angel name)

8.

To be drawn 3 times over the alpha chakra one hand length below base of the spine
Veleechsbikluatret
Creating movement in light

angel sigil:

Call in the angel: Belech-his-pavatra
(look at the angel sigil while calling angel name)

Also call in the angel Kelipretvaha *for placing this sigil into the earth.*

9.

To be drawn 3 times over the bottom of each foot
Nunmerstararotbelchspi
Bringing in the new template of frequency

angel sigil:

Call in the angel: Kretna-ulu-vesbi
(look at the angel sigil while calling angel name)

(Figure 68)

216

Initiation Mastery Level III

This sigil is not to be used on patients.
It is for initiation of practitioners only.

Belveresnukvi
All becomes One

Do three times over each of the following: (in order given)

1. bottom of each foot

2. alpha chakra

3. root chakra

4. lower abdomen

5. navel

6. solar plexus

7. heart

8. sternum

9. throat

10. forehead

11. crown

12. both hands

13. 10" above crown

angel name: Urhetvi

angel sigil:

(Figure 69)

217

Closing Sigils to End a Session

Praise

Love

Gratitude

(Figure 70)

218

Earth. The master sigil extends this influence to the whole cosmos. *(See Fig. 65-71, Initiation Sigils for Belvaspata)*

After having practiced the sigils regularly and above all, having internalized the true emotions and rays of light, a Level II practitioner becomes connected through this sigil to the grid of existence that spans the cosmos. Practicing Belvaspata, therefore, becomes a cosmic service, bringing healing to life everywhere.

Where great service is rendered, great rewards are given. The rewards in this instance are that the sigils previously placed in the centers of the practitioner's body during Level I and Level II initiations, now work 100 times more effectively as the master uses them. A second magnificent reward is higher consciousness for the practitioner and greater silence of the mind, which is mastery.

Disease as an Illusion

Initiates into Belvaspata must very clearly understand why disease and the false emotions of anger, fear, pain and protectiveness are, at this point, an illusion. The reminder that healing is but the removal of illusion needs to be done with every use of the sigils. To treat disease as a real adversary, is to strengthen illusion.

In 2005 the "real" part, the indwelling life of disease, was removed. To demonstrate this, if I put my pen on the table and one of the masters of the unseen realms removes the etheric or 'real' pen, it would no longer be real.

I can still pick up the pen and write with it, but some days I may not see it and then one day it will have disappeared altogether. It will, in fact, disappear even quicker if my thinking it is on the table were to stop.

Guidelines for Practitioners of Belvaspata Healing Modality

- Understand and be able to explain to an initiate the difference between a symbol and a sigil.
- You do not have to sign the angel sigils in the air—just look at them as you call their name.
- The sigils done (signed in the air) over the body parts and for initia-

tion—you do not have to memorize them, but can copy them either from a paper held in the left hand or you can place a paper over the area and trace the sigil with your finger.

- The sigils are drawn from left to right. Start at the upper left-hand corner. After that, the order is not crucial.
- The language used is a very high cosmic language used by the Mother Goddess.
- There should be at least a three-month time lapse between Level I and Level II initiations. There should be a six-month lapse between Level II, and Mastery, with use of the sigils at least twice a week.
- It has to be clearly understood that this modality does not work with energy and matter but rather with light and frequency. The modality has been brought forth to replace previous methods as a result of the change in cosmic laws of attraction that occurred August 11, 2006 in connection with the cosmic ascension.
  - With energy and matter, opposites now repel. Healing energy will therefore be rejected, whereas it was previously received.
  - With light and frequency, opposites now attract. Light will therefore be drawn to illusion, and frequency will be received in areas of distortion.
- Certification may be provided for initiated practitioners. You may charge the same as you do for other healing modalities. The only exchange I ask for from you and from those whom you train, is an acknowledgement that the information originated through me. If it would enhance the value of the modality in advertising, you may freely reprint any of the endorsements (or portions thereof) from the back of my books or my website.
- Provide training to initiates on how to change the old ways of 'sending energy' into the body, to using the 12 new pairs of emotional frequencies and expanded perception. They need to prepare for initiations by internalizing the new emotions and light as required for the specific level.

Level I

The requirement for Level I initiation is to study and internalize the 12 pairs of emotions previously given.

Self-Initiation

Belvaspata self-initiations can be done only in conjunction with the use of the alphabet of the Mother Goddess of Creation. (*Fig. 71, The Language of the Holy Mother)* In addition, the time periods between initiations previously stipulated, while the practitioner regularly uses the sigils, must be strictly observed.

The following steps must be taken, in order, for the self-initiation of Level I Belvaspata:

1. Carefully study the material previously written about this healing modality that has come from Mother, including how to heal with Belvaspata.

2. Set aside an eight-hour period to internalize the 12 pairs of emotional frequencies as given previously.

3. Write out the initiation as given in Mother's language (using her alphabet) from left to right, from top to bottom, in columns, leaving a space between words. Each initiation sigil and its wording in Mother's language must be on a separate page so that you can place it on a different body center.

4. When complete, lie down and place each sigil's drawing on the three different related body centers with the translation that has been done in Mother's language regarding that sigil.

5. Now read out loud in Mother's tongue what you have written as the initiations. Sign the sigils three times in the air.

6. Always end with the sigils for love, praise and gratitude, signed by you.

7. Send the original of this translation you have done, with the originals of the three sigils you have drawn, to a Belvaspata master of your choice.[95] Request that they issue you a certificate, and ask whether they will keep your file to work with issuing your certificates for initiations of Levels II and III as well. This is done so they can ensure observance of the time periods between initiations.

8. If the same master is not available for Levels II and III, send copies of your previous certificates to another, reflecting the dates they were issued.

95. See the Belvaspata website for a list.

The Language of the Holy Mother

Magic is in the
moment. (vursh
venes-tu par-
neshtu)

Great things
await.
(Iuvishpa
niutrim sarem)

Let the fun
begin.
(Ruftra-
vasbi iulem)

Please take me with
you. (Nun brash bar-
nut pareshvi)

(Figure 71)

222

The Initiations—Level I

Self-Initiation

Pelech vi brashvata urespi klaunash strechvi uklesva uhuru reshvi straunach Belvaspata. (The same words are spoken for the initiation of the self or another.)

By the power of the holy language, I enter into the Level 1 initiation of Belvaspata.

1. *Uklesh varabi ukretnet **Rutsetviurubach** u palva uheristat kletvubra. Kre stubava uset uvechvi kraunat valavish usta vabi uretvi **Blautvapata** pre nusvi haruhit.*

    For the opening of my mind, I call in the angel **Rutsetviurubach**. By the power of his sigil, I instruct him to place the sigil of **Blautvapata** three times on my forehead.

2. *Uklesh varabi ukretnet **Iornumubach** u varespi uheristat kletvubra. Kre stubava uset uvechvi kraunat valavish usta vabi varespi **Kruvechpaururek** pre nusvi haruhit.*

    For the opening of my heart, I call in the angel **Iornumubach**. By the power of his sigil I instruct him to place the sigil of **Kruvechpaururek** three times in my heart.

3. *Uklesh varabi ukretnet **Truararirpleva** u stavavechspi umirarat. Kre stubava uset uvechvi kraunat valavish usta vabi pres pranatuk **Kelavisbavah** pre nusvi haruhit. Esta u manurch bria stuvaba reshvi straunach Belvaspata.*

    For the receptivity of the body, I call in the angel **Truararirpleva**. By the power of his sigil I instruct him to place the sigil of **Kelavisbavah** three times within my navel. I am now in Level I Belvaspata.

(See Fig. 65, Initiation Sigils Level I and Fig. 70, Closing Sigils to End a Session)

(Figs. 72 –74, Sigils of Love)

223

Sigils of Love*

**These sigils are used in pairs to stimulate healthy frequency.
To be used by Level I Belvaspata practitioners.**

1.
+

−

Love/Angel name:
Perechpriparva

Trust/Angel name:
Truessabruvarabi

*use for obesity
and flab*

2.
+

−

Inspiration/Angel name:
Kriavatbishpi

Peace/Angel name:
Pelenanvabruk

*use in areas of
red rash, redness,
or inflamation*

3.
+

−

Creativity/Angel name:
Velesvruchba

Pleasure/Angel name:
Prubechbanatruva

*genitals,
reproductive
organs*

4.
+

−

Empathy/Angel name:
Felvirespiuhuruvak

Acknowledgement/Angel name:
Treuchvaravaar

injuries

* *Initiates for Level II need to prepare for a day by internalizing these emotions.*

(Figure 72)

5.

+

−

Generosity/Angel name:
Teshvinechspiurarat

Receptivity/Angel name:
Nenhurshbrechbravit

*used to reduce
blood pressure*

6.

+

−

Encouragement/Angel name:
Kletsutvesba

Beauty/Angel name:
Nunbereshnuk

*pancreas, liver,
gallbladder*

7.

+

−

Communication/Angel name:
Araragatveshpi

Assimilation/Angel name:
Nunhereshvispi

lungs

8.

+

−

Passion/Angel name:
Gelkrigsutvrabararech

Joy/Angel name:
Travi-usbava

*use for poor
circulation*

(Figure 73)

9.

+

Achievement/Angel name:
Gelevishtrava

throat,
thyroid

–

Fun/Angel name:
Pru-eshbiklechvaha

10. +

Enlightenment/Angel name:
Grunachberesvik

use for pain

–

Contentment/Angel name:
Kletsatvarabuch

11. +

Empowerment/Angel name:
Buesbiklechnatra

digestive tract,
elimination,
kidneys, adrenals

–

Humor/Angel name:
Veluchvesprirekva

12. +

Growth/Angel name:
Trubikluvespraha

bones, fractures,
muscles, joints

–

Satisfaction/Angel name:
Nechtruavar

(Figure 74)

Level II

The requirement for Level II Initiation is to study and internalize the following sixteen Rays of Light.

Embodying The Sixteen Rays of Light

The root of Light is the Infinite; the Goddess Mother of all Creation. She is like the white light that splits into colors. In the new creation into which we have entered, there are sixteen rays of light that move throughout existence. Although our minds may not initially grasp and interpret that we are seeing colors never before seen, we are nevertheless in a new color spectrum. Previously, light reflected the static gridwork of the cosmos; now it reflects cosmic movement.

The Sixteen Rays in a Clockwise Position

1. **The Root**—During this cycle of existence, Mother, the Source of all light, is the root of light. The purity and incorruptible nature of Her Being henceforth safeguards the Cosmic Light against distortion.

   As we seek to internalize the root of light in our lives, let us be always mindful that we exist in the holiness of Her Being and that we can dedicate every action, every breath we take in love, praise and gratitude to the One Being that sustains us and gives us life.

   In meditation, let us see ourselves become as vast as the cosmos and as we linger there, let us know we have become one with the Infinite Mother—that in such expanded awareness, we are being cradled in Her loving arms. It is here where we will find the Source of all light.

2. **Faith**—The nature of faith has changed for this creation. Formerly, it was a mindset that re-created itself. In other words, the most prevalent and dominant thoughts ended up creating our environment. Because our thoughts were generally chaotic, we created chaotic conditions on Earth.

   The new creations do not come through thought, but through the heart. We create through love, praise and gratitude—a way that prevents us from creating more chaos. Faith, as a way to create our reality, has to therefore reflect this change.

The new way to understand faith would be as the conscious creation of reality through an attitude of love. Envision how you would like to live life, and flood the images with love, praise and gratitude that such joyous manifestations can be yours.

3. Balance—The light-ray of balance represents the essence of what the Mayans call 'Movement and Measure.' Balance is not static, but rather consists of the dynamic movement between expanding boundaries. In other words, it moves between positive and negative aspects within existence, always pulling them slightly further apart.

As an example, a balanced life pulses between beingness and doingness. The deeper we enter into the peace of our being, the more we can accomplish with our actions (our 'doingness'). In this way, both our passive and pro-active aspects are strengthened and enhanced. In these deepening pulsations, lies the expansion and growth of the being.

4. Abundance—The true meaning of abundance has been colored by the beautiful and uplifting purpose of our new existence, creation through the heart. Before, we hoped that life would deliver abundance. Now we are limited only by how large we can dream and how much love we can pour into our dreams and visions.

While doing this, we continue to broadcast heartfelt gratitude throughout the cosmos for what we have. Increases do not occur where there is an absence of gratitude for present gifts. Conversely, whatever we are grateful for increases.

Generosity also increases supply. If we truly understand that we are co-creators of our realities, then our supply has no limit. In giving, we simply open the sluices of manifestation a little wider. If we have love, praise and gratitude, we open it wider still; clustering awareness into manifesting our created realities.

5. Wisdom—It has been said that wisdom is applied knowledge. Previously, we had to interpret principles that lay hidden within the illusion of the former cycle of existence. Now all illusion has been solved and the new creation lies before us like a pristine uncharted land. What knowledge is there to apply?

The knowledge that needs to be interpreted through our lives is the knowledge of self we see mirrored within those of like energy. In them, we see ourselves and learn about what we are. Learning by observing those energies in others, we become more of what we are and find new ways of applying them in our lives.

6. Mercy—Mercy no longer means tolerating the dysfunctional in our midst. In fact, the opposite is true. Because opposite light and frequency (emotion) now attract, the most merciful way of living is to surround ourselves with authentic, love-filled people who make our hearts sing. As we feel joy, it is automatically drawn to its opposite aspect, the most joyless places in the cosmos.

Mercy therefore resembles a form of 'tough love,' a refusal to indulge the clinging to old patterns of illusion as some will want to do. The repelling of those of opposite energies used to be considered 'uncharitable'—now not living our highest truth is.

7. Diversity—The greatest period of growth for any group of beings is when there is unity within diversity, creating interdependency. The slowest growth, and ultimately stagnation, occurs when there is uniformity. We see this in tribal life. The dynamic within the group is one of dependency, keeping its members in an infantile state.

Because the new creation stresses 'sameness,' diversity within the 'sameness' is absolutely vital. If this were not the case, the possibility of over-polarization into the known (accessed light) would be a very real concern. The inevitable result of such over-polarization is stagnation.

Although we are to study the beautiful qualities of others, we are in fact studying our own. We can only recognize that which we have within—the major reason why light-promoters have been so easily deceived by those of ill-intent. Although what we see is what we are, every other person is like a uniquely colored lens through which his beam of light shines. When this diversity is observed and appreciated, it brings richness to our lives.

8. Energy—The deep secret behind this fact is that matter and energy have merged. This has already occurred. The gods and goddesses in human form have become 100% energy and are moving into becoming an even more refined form of light.

A whole new reality is being born, one in which the Mother Goddess Herself will reign on this most pivotal planet, Earth.

9. Bliss—Bliss is a result of a vast expansive perception that effects the vibration of a body's cells. It is a state of profound praise, love and gratitude generated by an eternal perspective.

The gift of bliss is that old patterns melt away in its presence; constrictions in the flow of energy release. Others experience healings and growth by grace. In a new creation where we are able to access awareness by grace through the ascension attitudes, bliss is more readily present. As one of the rays of light, it offers growth through grace and births hope that anyone can achieve the pinnacle of enlightenment through love, praise and gratitude.

10. Perception—Perception used to come through the gifts of challenge and hardship. Through the friction of life's experiences turning the unknown into the known, perception exacted a high cost.

In the cycle of existence just completed, perception yielded emotion as the primary way of promoting change. Perception birthed the realities of our lives. In this creation, our emotions primarily steer our course, affecting our perception. The more profound our emotions, the more they birth our hopes and dreams into reality.

Imagine our lives as a sphere of existence filled with twelve concentric circular frequency bands (emotion). If the emotions strengthen, the bands expand. Light rays bounce through these bands. If they expand, the light rays have to move through a larger sphere; therefore they have to move faster to complete their pattern. The more intense the emotion, the faster we get our perception.

11. Presence—The Mother of All has a specific 'flavor' to Her light—a personality that expresses Her Being in this cycle of Creation more than any other. Within this ray of light, the presence of the Infinite Divine Being is accessed and known.

The stillness of Mother's ancient moments, timeless and eternal, the tempestuousness of her cataclysmic change, all can be felt through this ray. The reflections of the facets of Her Being are reflected in the stupendous variety and exquisite beauty of Her creations. We can study the Mother's being by seeing Her face in the reflections of the cosmos.

The study and interpretation of the majesty and glory of the Infinite Mother is really the study of self. We are Her facets, her reflections. We can only recognize in Her what we are in ourselves. This creation is dedicated to studying the known, that which we are, by accessing it within the divine presence of the Mother of Creation.

12. **Hope**—Hope is a state of mind that lives with eyes and heart firmly fixed on the most beneficial outcome. Hope has taken on an entirely new meaning since our reason for being has become creation of that which we love through the heart.

Hope is the vision we hold as we fan the flame of its creation through love, praise and gratitude. This acts upon the substance of things hoped for, formed from tiny fragments of awareness that have always existed, but have now become abundantly available for us to create with.

An attitude is comprised of both love and light. The attitudes of ascension are really the positively charged aspects of awareness. The awareness particles comprise the opposite (negative) aspect. Awareness also consists of both love (frequency) and light (where opposites attract), The little rays rush towards the source of the ascension attitudes. Here they roll, cluster and fill the mold created by hope.

13. **Mastery**—Mastery advocates a life lived from complete authenticity, self-discipline, and inner balance. Mastery is a combination of many attributes that take dedication and focus to achieve. Previously these attributes took years to cultivate, one painstaking step at a time.

With awareness immediately available and with time's collapse into the moment, mastery is now at our fingertips. It takes a mindset that always acts from our highest vision, remembering that we are a vast being superimposed over all that is and that wherever we are is the center of our cosmos.

Mastery acts with the utmost impeccability and sensitivity in realizing that every action, every thought impacts the whole. With such awareness, each act becomes an act of love for the interconnectedness of all life.

14. **Discovery**—The great significance of the introduction of this ray of light into Creation is as follows:

• The previous cycles of creation were descension cycles, containing a great deal of distorted light. The descension was due to self-centered and separative patriarchal rule. This distorted emotion created fear, anger, pain and protectiveness. Thus we were driven further and further down into density.

• It did not have to be this way. Mother had given freedom of choice to Her creations. The choices of Mother's creations brought about these painful descension cycles and ultimate rebellion and destruction.

• The way it was meant to be was through joyful discovery of the unknown, much the same way the ancient mariners set forth to explore the uncharted seas. It was supposed to be a treasure hunt—finding the gems within our being lying in the dust of the unknown. Through many of the choices made by the higher gods, the adventure of discovery became a nightmare.

The reinstallation of this precious ray of light is a wonderful gift as we study the known.

15. **Power**—In the new creation, all of the previous rays of light moved into the ray of Power, which then moved to birth the 16th ray, as follows:

• All previous rays moved into the one ray, namely the ray of Power.
• The one ray of Power then moved into the inner emotional sphere of trust/love with the brilliance of all fifteen rays.
• The great power and light caused the emotional sphere to spin counterclockwise.

How the Cosmos Formed

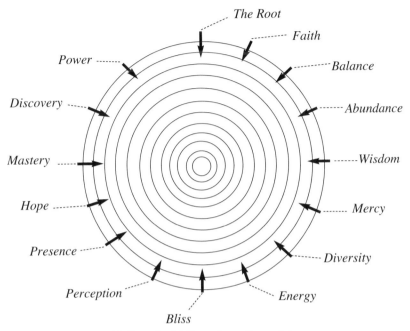

Initially only 15 Rays form through tones.

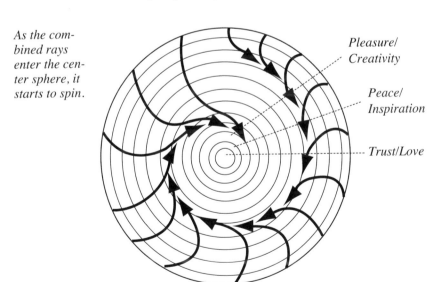

As the combined rays enter the center sphere, it starts to spin.

The 15 Rays take shape at the edge of the cosmic womb but bend in a clockwise direction, becoming one as they enter the sphere of Trust.

(Figure 75)

233

Continued: How the Cosmos Formed

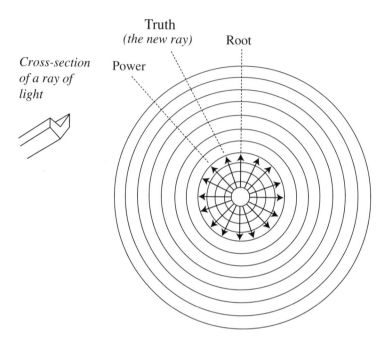

Center sphere is spinning and shoots out 16 Rays.
The new 16th Ray of truth is born.

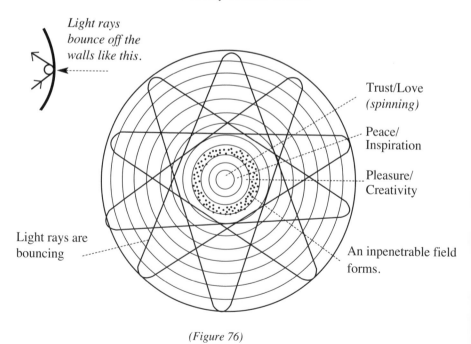

(Figure 76)

Continued: How the Cosmos Formed

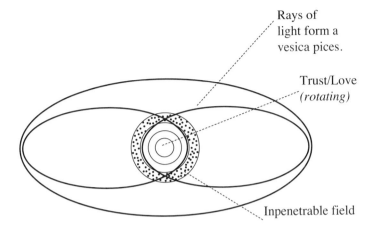

Rays of
light form a
vesica pices.

Trust/Love
(rotating)

Inpenetrable field

The twelve rings are stretched into an oval.

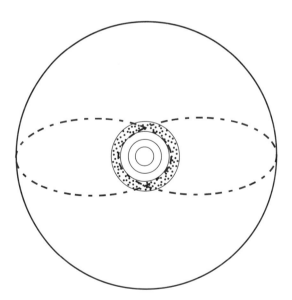

The rings enlarge to form perfect spheres again. Expansion results.

(Figure 77)

Sixteen Rays of Light Moving in the Cosmos

These need to be internalized for Level II Belvaspata initiations

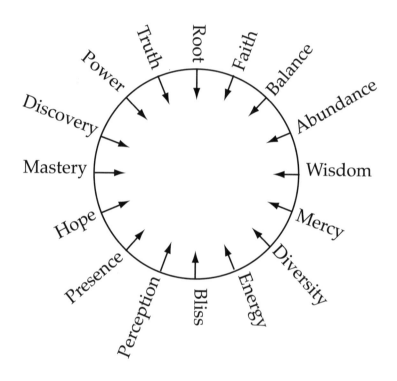

The sixteen rays of light, representing certain attributes, bounce off the border of the cosmos. In the new cosmic cycle, light moves and emotional frequency bands and awareness are static.

(Figure 78)

• The rapid spinning shot out all fifteen previous rays plus an additional one, a pink ray embodying absolute truth.

The first fifteen rays previously mentioned had originally been meant to become available as the cosmos ascended. This would have provided the cosmos the ability to move on to a new existence beyond (as we have just done) without having to go through numerous and repetitive cycles of ascension and decension. Due to the distortion chosen by some of the lords of the light rays at the very pinnacle of existence, the additional rays were never given by the Mother of Creation until now. *(See Figs. 75–77, How the Cosmos Formed and Fig. 78, Sixteen Rays of Light Moving in the Cosmos)*

16. **Truth**—This newly born ray of truth is a new form of this principle. Truth was previously that which was sought without, though the phantoms of illusion, clustered about us, attracted to our light. Truth is no longer found without—after all, we are in a play that has yet to be written. There are no preconceived guidelines here. It lies before us, pristine as this newborn ray of truth. This ray is the firstborn child of the cosmos; it is to be felt in our hearts as *The Ring of Truth*.

Level II —Self-Initiation

After spending a day internalizing the sixteen rays of light previously given, perform the Level II self-initiation in the same way as previously done for Level I.

Pelech vi brashvata urespi klaunash strechvi uklesva basetvi reshvi straunach Belvaspata.

By the power of the holy language, I enter into the Level II initiation of Belvaspata.

1. *Uklesh varabi ukretnet **Krunechva-atruha** u stechvabi uleska bret net hurava. Kre stubava uset uvechvi kraunat valavish usta vabi perenutvi skaulag **Kelavisva-uravech** pre nusvi haruhit.*

   For the release of patterns that no longer serve, I call in the angel **Krunechva-atruha**. By the power of his sigil I instruct him to place the sigil of **Kelavisva-uravech** three times in my lower abdomen.

2. *Uklesh varabi ukretnet **Mirakluvael** u ste u plavaa urechspi hersh-stavaa uknech staura. Kre stubava uset uvechvi kraunat valavish usta vabi keres nusta-ava **Trechsubareshvi** pre nusvi haruhit.*

   For the transmuting of matter to energy and then to light, I call in the angel **Mirakluvael**. By the power of his sigil I instruct him to place the sigil of **Trechsubareshvi** three times in my solar plexus.

3. *Uklesh varabi ukretnet **Kelevitraunar** u trana uruvet pre usta utvi us plavaa. Kre stubava uset uvechvi kraunat valavish usta vabi krune-spi ustava **Patauruhutvi** pre nusvi haruhit.*

   For the transfiguring of illusion to light, I call in the angel **Kelevitraunar**. By the power of his sigil I instruct him to place the sigil of **Patauruhutvi** three times in my sternum.

4. *Uklesh varabi ukretnet **Trechbaruruheresvi** u stavavechspi pre uhus traurat. Kre stubava uset uvechvi kraunat valavish usta vabi brat nutva rechspanadoch **Kersbaurveshpi** pre nusvi haruhit.*

   For the sanctification of the body I call in the angel **Trechbaruruheresvi**. By the power of his sigil I instruct him to place the sigil of **Kersbaurveshpi** three times in my crown.

5. *Uklesh varabi ukretnet **Vilivesbikeresna** u sta binavich steretu uvlaesh kletvubra. Kre stubava uset uvechvi kraunat valavish usta vabi stiek-luava uprech vabi **Kletsutmanarech** pre nusvi haruhit.*

   For the attracting of light into my voice, I call in the angel **Vilivesbikeresna**. By the power of his sigil I instruct him to place the sigil of **Kletsutmanarech** three times in my throat.

6. *Uklesh varabi ukretnet **Kruechnavilshpreva** u bestich haru vereshva kletvubra. Kre stubava uset uvechvi kraunat valavish usta vabi peresnustavat kliechspi **Visbelespahrechvi** pre nusvi haruhit.*

   For the attracting of healing energies into my hands, I call in the angel **Kruechnavilshpreva**. By the power of his sigil I instruct him to place the sigil of **Visbelespahrechvi** three times in my right hand.

7. *Uklesh varabi ukretnet **Kruechnavilshpreva** u bestich haru vereshva kletvubra. Kre stubava uset uvechvi kraunat valavish usta vabi peresnustavat truvachspi **Visbelespahrechvi** pre nusvi haruhit.*

238

For the attracting of healing energies into my hands, I call in the angel **Kruechnavilshpreva**. By the power of his sigil I instruct him to place the sigil of **Visbelespahrechvi** three times in my left hand.

8. *Uklesh varabi ukretnet **Ku-uluvet** stau nenhurpersh ustachni versh u stanavach steraa. Kre stubava uset uvechvi kraunat valavish usta vabi tremish uretkla uvra vesti pelenuch ustechbi **Nenhershbikletrasut** pre nusvi haruhit.*

   For the DNA activation of the codes of light, I call in the angel **Ku-uluvet**. By the power of his sigil I instruct him to place the sigil of **Nenhershbikletrasut** three times into my root chakra at the base of my spine.

9. *Uklesh varabi ukretnet **Belech-hispavatra** ukresh mi hes vi ustachva plavaa. Kre stubava uset uvechvi kraunat valavish usta vabi sta u achva usbanadoch sterut **Vele-echsbikluatret** pre nusvi haruhit. Uklesh baurabi ukretnet pehera **Kelipretvaha** tre u stamamit selbi usvi trevaa.*

   For the creation of movement in light, I call in the angel **Belech-hispavatra**. By the power of his sigil I instruct him to place the sigil of **Vele-echsbikluatret** three times in the alpha chakra (one hand length below the base of the spine).

   I ask that his wife **Kelipretvaha**, place the same sigil in the Earth.

10. *Uklesh varabi ukretnet **Kretnauluvesbi** paurivi heshva ustevavi klasutbaru uraesh. Kre stubava uset uvechvi kraunat valavish usta vabi kresna stechvi kliechspi **Nunmerstararotbelchspi** pre nusvi haruhit.*

    For the bringing in the new template of frequency, I call in the angel **Kretnauluvesbi**. By the power of his sigil I instruct him to place the sigil **Nunmerstararotbelchspi** three times into the bottom of my right foot.

11. *Uklesh varabi ukretnet **Kretnauluvesbi** paurivi hesva ustevavi klatsutbaru uraesh. Kre stubaba uset uvechvi kraunat valavish usta vabi kresna stechvi truvachspi **Nunmerstararotbelchspi** pre nusvi haruhit.*

    For bringing in the new template of frequency I call in the angel **Kretnauluvesbi**. By the power of his sigil I instruct him to place the sigil **Nunmerstararotbelchspi** three times into the bottom of my left foot.

Sigils of Light*

Can be used in a circle. Place sigils in order clockwise.

1.

Root/Lord name:
Herhutbrasta

always use in conjunction with other sigils of light

2.

Faith/Lord name:
Belblutvakreshbi

systemic illness

3.

Balance/Lord name:
Kluch-nenuvit

ears, throat, nose

4.

Abundance/Lord name:
Petrevusbi

prostate, rectum

5.

Wisdom/Lord name:
Gelviveshbi

pineal, hypothalamus

6.

Mercy/Lord name:
Truavar

spine, occipital area/base of skull

7.

Diversity/Lord name:
Pluakbar

DNA, chromosomes, memory

* *Initiates for Level II need to prepare for a day by internalizing these qualities.*

(Figure 79)

Continued: Sigils of Light

8.

Energy/Lord name:
Trechvarvulesbi

*blood sugar,
blood purification*

9.

Bliss/Lord name:
Besbrakva

*cellular light,
oxygen and ph of cells*

10.

Perception/Lord name:
Telenuchvraha

*eyes, pituitary,
3rd eye*

11.

Presence/Lord name:
Klechsavra

legs and feet

12.

Hope/Lord name:
Telerutskrava

*heart,
circulation*

13.

Mastery/Lord name:
Brishnavak

*brain, clarity of
thought*

14.

Discovery/Lord name:
Verebisma

*tongue, teeth,
tonsils*

(Figure 80)

Continued: Sigils of Light

15.

Power/Lord name:
Veruchmavaheshbi

skull, scalp, hair

16.

Truth/Lord name:
Petluchvraha

*arms, elbows,
hands/wrists,
shoulders*

Use for Emotional Health

depression

Angel: Nechvikrechbar

(Figure 81)

*Esta u vish basetvatu reshvi straunach Belvaspata esba unavespi
stechmanarot ra utvaba kelesvi unus kraunata pre us ubarech.*

I am now initiated into Level II of Belvaspata and connected to the
planetary grid to bring healing through the use of these sigils.

(See Figs. 66–68 on pages 214–216, Initiation Sigils Level II) and *(Fig.
79–81, Sigils of Light)*

Master Level

The requirement for Master Level initiation is to study and internalize
the 12 States of Being.

The Twelve Pure States of Being

1. **Praise (+)** As a state of being it is slightly different than when it is an
   attitude. Attitudes have more perception. Praise is the surge of deep,
   exultant feeling that comes from accessing the highest aspect within.
   It is the triumph of recognizing the perfection underlying appearances.
   Glory (-) Is the maintenance of the highest aspect of ourselves as a
   being as vast as the cosmos, and its expression in our lives. In other
   words, it is when we live life from our largest perspective.

2. **Exploration (+)** Is the pushing beyond previous boundaries of
   expression so that new creation and deeper expression can take place
   for the sake of growth.
   Harmony (-) Is the state of being resulting from being in step with
   the blueprint or will of the Infinite; when smaller segments of
   Creation express synchronistically with the largest purpose of life.

3. **Gratitude (+)** This state of being results from encountering the true
   nature of the cosmos as one that supports all life, the recognition of
   the nurturing of the Divine in our lives.
   Guidance (-) The revelation of the most life-enhancing choices
   along our path and the uncovering of the blueprint of our existence.
   (**Note:** Within the irrevocable overall purpose of our lives there are
   now more choices and freedom of expression available than ever as

we enter our spiritual maturity.)

4. **Discernment (+)** Although all unknown portions of Mother's being have been solved during the cycles of the Fall, there is nevertheless always a mystery as to which expression of the known portions of Her being would be most life-enhancing. The discernment comes when our hearts reveal this mystery.

   Transparency (-) Is the revelation of a portion of existence that reflects the purity of absolute truth.

5. **Understanding (+)** When we regard our true identity as a being as vast as the cosmos, all is **within** our consciousness that is **without** our bodies. Understanding comes when the light fibers within our bodies light up, or come on line, as a result of something outside our bodies revealing its information.

   Reflection (-) When something is encountered in life that evokes an emotional response, it is worthy of study and further scrutiny. It is an indicator of whether we have lived our highest truth. It may also be an indicator of a mystery waiting to reveal itself. Reflection will show whether what we have understood is worthy of implementing and incorporating into our life.

6. **Embrace (+)** Is the reaching to incorporate more of the vastness of existence into our compassionate understanding and acceptance.

   Ecstasy (-) Results from the inclusiveness of our vision that sees each life as its own.

7. **Manifestation (+)** Fifty percent[96] of life is ours to manifest and create at will; that part of life in which we can creatively contribute to the big picture. Manifestation occurs when awareness clusters itself into the circumstances of our lives, pulled forth by the emotions of our hearts as well as our attitudes.

   Inevitability (-) Each of us plays a part in contributing to the growth and evolution of the large plan or pattern of life. This constitutes inevitability: the experiences we are required to live according to our mutual contract with the Infinite. Because growth comes through

96. As of May 2007.

mutual support, the large plan also writes in some 'key moments' — moments of support that are given in our own lives depending on which choices we make. This is part of the set circumstances, of inevitability, in our lives.

8. **Oneness (+)** Living the deep awareness that all beings are part of us makes us aware of the interconnectedness of life. We gain this understanding by opening ourselves to include all parts of existence.
   Contentment (-) This results when oneness occurs and life flows through us without obstruction. We feel that we have come home.

9. **Integration (+)** The praiseworthy parts of life beckon for us to make them our own—to integrate them as a part of us. That which we find unworthy of integrating, nevertheless has gifts in the form of insights that are worth making our own and should not be dismissed.
   Evolution (-) As the caterpillar grows with each bite of the leaf it eats, so we grow in depth of wisdom and perception with each part of our experiential learning we make our own and integrate. Change for the better is therefore the one constant in a life well-lived.

10. **Play (+)** The spontaneous and lighthearted interaction with the unexpected creates a useful flexibility. It spontaneously and abundantly creates a grace and ease of interaction with life in the moment.
    Flexibility (-) The cumbersome weight of self-reflection, self-pity and self-importance weighs down the journey and keeps us locked into points of view. Any viewpoint could, in the next moment, be obsolete as life changes constantly, thought by thought.

11. **Perception (+)** Much abuse of power has occurred by reversing the polarity of power and perception. Power is the state of being that results from perception, not the other way around. It is perception that must actively be sought in our world, not power.
    Power (-) Power as a feminine pole is vastly more powerful than power that is masculine and separative. Power that is feminine, and therefore inclusive in nature, is the power that is aligned with all that is.

12. **Retention (+)** To retain or allow something to flow through our lives requires our making a simple choice. The only real question in all

existence is what is life-enhancing and what is not. That which is, we retain as our own.

Conductivity (-) Conductivity when fully lived, brings our lives into a state of grace. The alternative, resistance to that which we choose not to retain, leaks energy and lowers consciousness. It embodies the complete surrender to life.

Master Level—Self-initiation

Again, Steps 1 through 8 in Level I are followed. There is only one Master Sigil and only one page of translation (if it runs over onto more than one page, staple them together), but the sigil drawings must be placed three times on each of the chakras, with the translation one time on each chakra.[97] A day must be set aside in preparation, internalizing the twelve states of being.

Uklesh tre basetvi me uspata reshvi berek nautar Belvaspata, uklesh varabi ukretnet nautari spa uvechvi **Belveresnukvi**. *Kre stubavat usetvi sta unava,* **Urhetvi** *kreunes tra va esta ulvavech ustavravi es bautra pre nusvi haruhit esbaerch usmi treur nun hesvata.*

Uset uvechvi steba kresna stechvi kliechspi esba u stau vi kresna stechvi truvachspi.Uset uvechvi steba achva usbanadoch sterut es vra tremish uretkla esva perenutvi skaulag. Uset uvechvi pres pranatuk es keres nustaava esva varespi esva krunespi ustava. Uset uvechvi steba stiekluava uprech vabi esba uretvi esba brat nutva rechspanadoch esba peresnustavat kliechspi esba peresnustavat truvachspi. Uset uvechvi steba stabalut.

Lahun estakva knues bra us ta uvi brat rechspanadoch. Parus na ta esva klua nu Lahun. Esta u vish basetvu reshvi pelevradoch ukles parva Belvaspata esbaur ne tru bravabit basetvi kluavanet perhet pra usva kliunesvi eshtra usbava Amanur.

For my initiation into the maste level of Belvaspata, I call in the angel of the master sigil, **Belveresnukvi**. By the power of your sigil that I hold, **Urhetvi** come forth and place this sigil that connects me to the cos-

---

97. Once the original is done, copies can be used to place on chakras.

mic grid three times in each of the centers I mention.

Place it into the bottom of my left foot and the bottom of my right foot.

Place it into my alpha chakra (one hand length below the base of the spine) and my root chakra and my lower abdomen.

Place it into my navel and my solar plexus and my heart and my sternum.

Place it into my throat and my forehead and my crown and my right hand and my left hand.

Place it into the tenth chakra ten inches above my crown, known as the Lahun.

Let all become one and one become all. I am now initiated as a Master of Belvaspata and am able to initiate others into this sacred healing modality given by the Mother Goddess of All Creation. *(See Fig. 69 on pg. 217, Initiation Mastery Level III)*

Sigils of the Twelve States of Being
as used in Belvaspata

1. Praise (+)	Glory (-)	Use
Angel – *Kuluheshpiuvrata*		To increase awareness by infusing the blood stream with awareness particles.

2. Exploration (+)	Harmony (-)	Use
Angel – *Grustervirabach*		To clear neuro-pathways and enhance the perception of subtle information.

3. Integration (+)	Evolution (-)	Use
Angel – *Kruapretparva*		To balance the tones of all the bodies of man.

4. Discernment (+)	Transparency (-)	Use
Angel – *Nunheshbielstuavet*		For the integration of all nine levels of light as information.

(Figure 82)

5. Understanding (+)	Reflection (-)	Use

Angel –
Brashechnetvetparva

For the excretion of higher hormones to evolve the physical body.

6. Play (+)	Flexibility (-)	Use

Angel –
Gertraskuvaelenustraberechnit

For the evolving of the DNA to the next stages of evolution.

7. Perception (+)	Power (-)	Use

Angel –
Pelenichvrausetbi

Opening the doorways of potential.

8. Embrace (+)	Ecstasy (-)	Use

Angel –
Grustachvauveshbi

For the connection with the Infinite Mother to be established.

(Figure 83)

Sigils of the Twelve States of Being
as used in Belvaspata Continued

9. Manifestation (+)	Inevitability (-)	Use
Angel – *Gelstraubechspi*		For the expression and interpretation of full potential.

10. Gratitude (+)	Guidance (-)	Use
Angel – *Vertlusbraveparhut*		For the awakening of the inner hearing and clairaudience.

11. Oneness (+)	Contentment (-)	Use
Angel – *Sutbiuvechbiklausetvaruach*		For the removal of any obstacles to clairvoyance and the awakening of second sight.

12. Retention (+)	Conductivity (-)	Use
Angel – *Viresklachbirestna*		For the release of any blockages of perception in the higher bodies.

(Figure 84)

The Grand Master Level of Belvaspata

Introduction

Since the first hours of receiving this most sacred healing modality, a gift from the Mother, I have known that although we were initially given the Level I, Level II and Master Levels, a Grand Master Level would be forth coming.

Belvaspata's first three levels are meant to beneficially impact the physical, etheric, emotional, and mental bodies of beings only. Likewise, at Level II the four lower bodies of the planet are impacted. At the Master Level, the four lower bodies of the cosmos are also affected by the sigils.

The Grand Master Level affects the spiritual emotional, spiritual mental and spirit bodies of all.

Grand Mastery promotes the coming together of life in the more subtle and physical levels of existence. With the large effort masters everywhere have been making to get Mother's Palace visible to all, every use of the sigils promotes this.

Because of the fact that in April 2007, man as a microcosm and also the cosmos as macrocosm, received two extra bodies, I suspect that at some point sigils will come forth that are to affect them also. Mother has implemented many steps to boost the evolution of man during the first few months of 2007. This has been done to create what She calls a 'super-charged human.' This level of Belvaspata removes obstructions that interfere with the opening and blossoming of the many new enhancements now found in that unique archetype – man.

There have been two impediments to Belvaspata working as immediately and fully as it is capable of:

1. There has been a thick membrane placed around physical life as mentioned in the Predictions of Isis. This has prevented the full capacity of the angelic assistance Belvaspata's sigils call in. It has of course also prevented great damage from being done to physical life. But with the dark ones removed as a threat, that membrane can now be opened. In order to do this, always place the Wheel given by Isis

(See Fig. 20 on page 76) which is a portal, on the client or in front of you when you work.

2. Secondly, the pollution of the light fibers of the spirit body caused by social conditioning, can obstruct the flow of light Belvaspata is designed to promote. Programming has therefore often stood in the way of the healing that is desired. The Grand Mastery level is gifted to us by the Mother to remove this interference within the higher bodies. *(See Fig. 85, The Seven Bodies of Man)*

Requisites for Receiving the Grand Master Level Initiation

1. The Master in Belvaspata needs to have practiced and used this healing modality regularly for at least six months.

2. The Twelve Heart Energies need to be internalized in exactly the same way that the emotions are in preparation for the Level I initiation. A full day needs to be set aside for this.

3. The Grand Master Level can be done through self-initiation, or it can be done through being initiated by another Grand Master.

4. An exception for the 6-month period between Mastery and Grand Mastery is only if the Master has silenced the internal dialogue of the mind, by being either in God-consciousness, Ascended Mastery (see the Stages of Man in *Secrets of the Hidden Realms*), or no longer in the human condition (the physical gods as spoken of by Isis). Under these circumstances, no waiting is necessary.

Comments

The Grand Master Level is the level for the immortality of the body. It is designed to release new hormones and open the higher capacities of the endocrine system. It connects the individual with assistance from the highest levels within the cosmos. It draws in additional angelic presences into our lives and brings clarity of mind and purity of heart as the pathways of light are cleared within the seventh body or spirit body. As it does so, it clears the cosmic pathways and removes old programming of suffering.

The Seven Bodies of Man

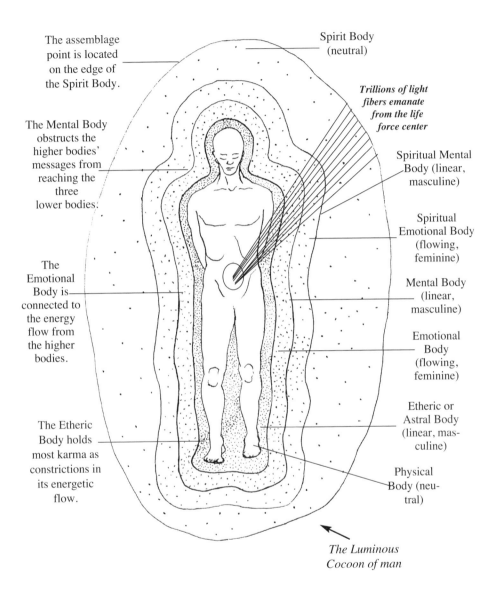

The assemblage point is located on the edge of the Spirit Body.

The Mental Body obstructs the higher bodies' messages from reaching the three lower bodies.

The Emotional Body is connected to the energy flow from the higher bodies.

The Etheric Body holds most karma as constrictions in its energetic flow.

Spirit Body (neutral)

Trillions of light fibers emanate from the life force center

Spiritual Mental Body (linear, masculine)

Spiritual Emotional Body (flowing, feminine)

Mental Body (linear, masculine)

Emotional Body (flowing, feminine)

Etheric or Astral Body (linear, masculine)

Physical Body (neutral)

The Luminous Cocoon of man

The bodies are superimposed over each other and form the luminous cocoon of man. The trillions of light fibers from the life force center penetrate all other bodies forming the spirit body.

(Figure 85)

253

Grand Master Level

The requirement for Master Level Initiation is to study and internalize the Twelve Heart Energies of the Zhong-galabruk.

Twelve Heart Energies

The twelve pairs of emotions combined with the 12 states of being interact to give the 12 heart energies

Emotions *and*	States of Being *give*	Heart Energies
Love (+)	Glory (-)	Ecstasy (+)
Trust (-)	Praise (+)	Embrace (-)
Inspiration (+)	Harmony (-)	Insight (+)
Peace (-)	Exploration (+)	Appreciation (-)
Creativity (+)	Guidance (-)	Inspiration (+)
Pleasure (-)	Gratitude (+)	Love (-)
Empathy (+)	Transparency (-)	Truth (+)
Acknowledgement (-)	Discernment (+)	Clarity (-)
Generosity (+)	Reflection (-)	Manifestation (+)
Receptivity (-)	Understanding (+)	Gratitude (-)
Encouragement (+)	Ecstasy (-)	Rejoicing (+)
Beauty (-)	Embrace (+)	Praise (-)
Communication (+)	Inevitability (-)	Harmony (+)
Assimilation (-)	Manifestation (+)	Wisdom (-)
Passion (+)	Contentment (-)	Fulfilment (+)
Joy (-)	Oneness (+)	Presence (-)
Achievement (+)	Evolution (-)	Growth (+)
Fun (-)	Integration (+)	Balance (-)
Enlightenment (+)	Flexibility (-)	Evolution (+)
Contentment (-)	Play (+)	Surrender (-)
Empowerment (+)	Power (-)	Discovery (+)
Humor (-)	Perception (+)	Awareness (-)
Growth (+)	Conductivity (-)	Acceptance (+)
Satisfaction (-)	Retention (+)	Allowing (-)

(Figure 86)

How the Emotions and States of
Being Intersect

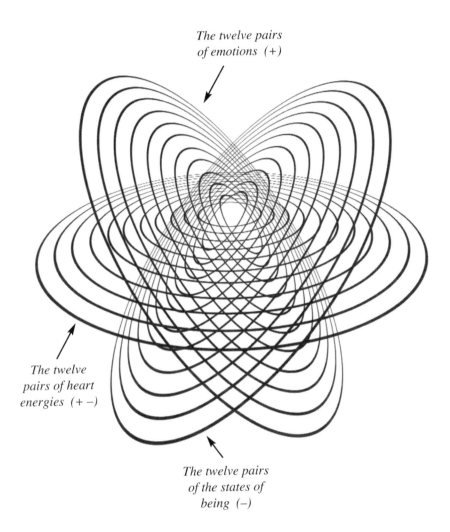

*The twelve pairs
of emotions (+)*

*The twelve
pairs of heart
energies (+ −)*

*The twelve pairs
of the states of
being (−)*

The rings each represent a pair that pulse between their positive and negative aspects. The wheels also pulse with one another. These are found not only as the grids of the cosmos, but around the body of man.

(Figure 87)

Preparation for the Grand Master Level
The Heart Energies from the Zhong-Galabruk

Heart energies are born when the emotions and the states of being pulse each other. This interaction produces particles of awareness that are a negative polarity in relation to the already existing awareness particles spread throughout the cosmos.

Awareness used to move until August of 2006 when massive changes occurred to the structure and nature of existence. Now awareness only moves in response to love, praise and gratitude as a magnetizing force. But the awareness particles emitted by the heart will vary from person to person, determined by his or her heart energies.

When there is an emission of these negative particles of awareness, they hover in that person's environment until directed to create through love, praise and gratitude, focused on a specific set of circumstances. As the cloud of awareness particles surrounds the person, these particles (although not moving directionally) vibrate. The dance, or vibration, of the particles is very much affected by the energetic qualities of the heart. When these particles dance in a similar way to someone else's, we can deduce that their heart energies are the same and that, since same energies attract, there will be a strong attraction.

Note: In August 2006, it was written by Mother in the Book of Life (which determines the laws of the cosmos), that heart energy will always be the determining factor (in other words stronger), rather than light or frequency in any relationship. In that way, light-workers will be attracted to one another, rather than have their similar light and frequencies repelling each other (remember: same light and frequency repel, same energies attract—the principles behind the effectiveness of Belvaspata as a healing method).

Explanation Of The Heart Energies

The quality of the heart energy is birthed by a masculine aspect and feminine aspect pulsing each other in an ongoing interaction. The deeper or stronger one aspect pulses, the deeper the other responds and the stronger the heart energy that is born.

1. Ecstasy(+) + Embrace(-) = Divine Compassion

Ecstasy as a positive factor is active: it is the broadcasting, or reaching out, of the ecstatic song of the heart. Wherever it reaches, the heart embraces; the heart includes in its compassionate embrace. Divine compassion can therefore be described as the ecstatic embrace of the heart.

2. Insight(+) + Appreciation(-) = Reverence

Insight, as a positive aspect, probes behind the illusion of appearances, finding the perfection underlying all life. True illusion as unsolved portions of existence no longer exist. All has been solved. But the "illusion" of taking things at face value continues. Insight refuses to take life at face value, finding the divine within. The response of the heart to seeing the divine order behind illusion is one of honoring and appreciation of life. From this vantage point, life is lived with reverence for all life, refining the person living this way and hallowing his experience.

3. Inspiration(+) + Love(-) = Pure Creativity

Inspiration is a positive quality, actively seeking out that which uplifts and inspires in what it observes. What uplifts and presents us with inspiration, evokes a deep love in our hearts. It creates a desire for us to be in its presence. The combination of the inspiration plus the love we feel for that which inspires, brings forth the desire to create through the heart— the place of pure creation.

4. Truth(+) + Clarity(-) = Absolute Truth

When truth, as we see it, is lived at its highest level, we start to express and live from a situation of clarity; where we are true, not only to others, but to ourselves. In clarity and truth we become aware of our motives' origins (Toltec mystics call it stalking ourselves). As we eliminate fear, protectiveness, anger and pain as motives, the reasons for taking action or making choices become clear and guides the promptings of our heart. The pure guidance of our heart comes from the blueprint of the Infinite (that which the Mother Goddess is) which is absolute truth.

5. Manifestation(+) + Gratitude(-) = Impeccability

The loss of impeccability is the result of failing to see the support of the greater scheme of our lives; of not recognizing that we are not alone. It is in thinking that we have to fend for ourselves that we act in a way that does not enhance the inter-connectedness of life. In allowing life's perfection to manifest in our lives in whatever way it wants to, and knowing with gratitude that we are sustained at all times, impeccability is born.

6. Rejoicing(+) + Praise(-) = Celebration

Rejoicing is a choice. It chooses to find that which is praiseworthy over that which is not. If one looks for that which is flawed, it is easy to find. Looking for that which one can rejoice in might take more work. In doing so, our life changes day by day into a song of praise, and transforms itself into one of celebration.

7. Harmony(+) + Wisdom(-) = Timing

There is a flow to life; subtle currents that determine the course of events. There is a time to act and a time to reflect; a time for output and a time for input. Our lives unfold with grace and in perfect timing when we have wisdom to stay in harmony with the soft whisperings of destiny. To have the wisdom to obey these inner whisperings, takes restraint. To hear them takes the silence of the mind of one who has ceased to oppose life.

8. Fulfillment(+) + Presence(-) = Focus

Toltec seers have given the sage advice to use death as an advisor; to live each moment as though it were our last, with the focus it deserves. The moment is the pivot point upon which all of life pivots. It is therefore that which holds life's potential. As such, it deserves our full presence so that it can yield its full potential. In other words, that moment can fulfill its promises of a new tomorrow, unfettered by yesterday's expectations. If tomorrow comes from the moment, but the moment is not lived in a fulfilling manner, with presence and focus, where will the future come from? It will instead be formed by our yesterdays, haphazardly and as a repeat of what went before.

9. Growth(+) + Balance(-) = Strength

Growth that is unsupported lacks strength. Growth is always tested, for gained knowledge has to become experiential knowledge to be truly useful. Without balance to bolster it, it will lack the strength to pass the testing of experience. Growth internally produces external change. If change is not balanced with rest, or our coming home to ourselves (more detailed information on Wings and Roots, audio CD by Almine), we will have wings but no roots. It is the dynamic pulsing between wings and roots that gives us our strength.

10. Evolution(+) + Surrender(-) = Grace

Grace is the enviable result of the ability of living with full cooperation with life. The surrender and trust of allowing life to evolve at its own pace, and in its own way, brings to our lives the grace of Mastery. It does not only require that we allow life to flow through us, but that we learn from it as it does, evolving through the insights it bestows.

11. Discovery(+) + Awareness(-) = Clarity

We have examined clarity in heart energy number 4, as the complete honesty with ourselves that requires a transparency of our motives. Clarity as an end result can be described as the certainty of what our next step is. The journey of existence becomes a journey of discovery when lived with the utmost awareness; an awareness born of the humility to know that only a fool can assume to know what the next moments will be. A life of clarity is not outcome oriented. It only knows that through living in the fullest awareness, the discovery of the next step will be achieved by living this one well, and thus a journey of clarity unfolds one step at a time.

12. Acceptance(+) + Allowing(-) = Harmlessness

Injury to life comes when we step out of contracts: when we fight and resist life's circumstances, keeping others and ourselves from growing. We often want life to change, but refuse to accept that we have to change ourselves. It is when we accept the moment for what it is, but allow change to come where it is needed by changing ourselves, that we fulfill life's contracts. Only then does life become empowered, rather than one of victimhood. When we feel life is out of control, we try to control its unfolding, causing harm to the interconnected web of life. By accepting our part of directing the play, but also allowing the script to unfold, life is lived harmlessly.

It is important that these 12 Pairs of Heart Energies should be studied and internalized in the same way as were the 12 Pairs of Emotions.

Grand Mastery

Self-Initiation

Steps 1 through 8 in Level I are followed, spending a day internalizing the twelve heart energies. The sigil drawing must be placed three times on the heart center with the page of translation into Mother's language and alphabet.

Barach usta hesvi klanevuk staba urechspi utklasvaba utrenuch steravik peleshba utklenevriavak uhes stau va klau nas prava uhuresbi. Esklat us ste uvra klenevash pra uvra kelesnut verek sta uvrabach usetvi minur pelesh **Bruakranuvigstela-u-achvraba, Kersh-heruvit-pele-achuvespiklauna, Stuapruanatvikeleshna** *et kla ninur varset pre us veleshbi ukletvi bre* **Kluagvanesvi-elu-achvrahereshviskaulag** *stunavek strau nas pra ve.*

Arvuklat vru elesbi sta minech staubileshvi usklaveres nesvabi ustech vre usbla eleshbi strau netvra stu velesbi nech tre ubrekva helesbi staravu. Kelvi arasva stu belechbi usta heresvri eshvra kluva vreshbi. Pre rech uvra nuresbi presatvi urla verleshvi Belvaspata kreunag viashva kluvanet **Kluagvanesvi-elu-achvrahereshviskaulag** *pre usutvi treunag mi uresh priesva kleunich.*

As one who has practiced this sacred healing of the heart with respect and in honor of all life, I present myself to become a grand master practitioner. I call the angels, **Bruakranuvigstela-u-achvraba, Kersh-heruvit-pele-achuvespiklauna** and **Stuapruanatvikeleshna**, and by the authority of their sigils, instruct them to place the grand mastery level sigil **Kluagvanesvi-elu-achvrahereshviskaulag** thrice in my heart center.

As grand master let them consecrate and initiate me, that I too may do so for others. Let my healing abilities increase one hundred fold. I am now a grand master of Belvaspata carrying the **Kluagvanesvi-elu-achvrahereshviskaulag** sigil within my heart.

The Grand Mastery Sigil

Kluagvanesvi–elu–achvraheresh–vi-skaulag

Three angels support this initiatory level

Brua–kranuvig–stela–u–achvraba

Kersh–heruvit–pele–ach–vespi–klauna

Stuapruanatvi–keleshna

(Figure 88)

Sigils that may be used by a Grand Master on a Client

1.
Stu–elavis–klauna   Angel: *Selvi–kluavak– heshpi*

For the removal of any obsolete programming from the
light fibers so that the light can be unobstructed in its flow

2.
Ersatvikeleshuava   Angel: *Kelibap-patrahesbi*

For the clear accessing and interpretation of potential

3.
Kri–ustavakrech-heresbi   Angel: *Stuavuhespi–echvravi*

For the production of awareness as co-creators of our lives

(Figure 89)

Sigils that may be used by a Grand Master on a Client

4.
Brabratkluvechspianuretvraha   Angel: *Belachveleshpavistuava–pranut*

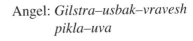

For the opening of the capacities for the next level of evolution

5.
Kulbelsta–uvachvakruneshvavi   Angel: *Gilstra–usbak–vravesh*
pikla–uva

For bringing the higher energies into the physical through
pulsing the states of being with the emotions

6.
Kelvikstauvavechspistraunak   Angel: *Barushbelechpa*

For the opening of the door of the pineal to receive awareness, and the
door of the heart to give awareness

(Figure 90)

Sigils that may be used by a Grand Master on a Client

7.

Stuabekbavak-klashvisprasteurit   Angel: *Tristarvamalvashnavek*

For the flow of information between the higher bodies
and the four lower bodies

8.

Vili–esvakluchbastuvechvabi   Angel: *Pritineshvakulu–esvabi*

For the constant awareness of our highest identity
as a never ending source of sustenance

9.

Beletrevahupspa–eravi   Angel: *Stuvaverehepshpikluanastrava*

For the development of interactive autonomy and sovereignty

(Figure 91)

The Tenth Sigil in the Tenth Chakra

Connecting the Bodies of Man to the Cosmic Bodies

The Lahun Sigil

Angel Name :
Harahuchparanechskava

By using this sigil above the head in the tenth chakra, the Grandmaster connects the person with the cosmic chakra for mutual support.

(Figure 92)

Placing the Ten Sigils for Healing
Used by Grand Masters

The cosmos benefits from the healing, and the person in
return receives cosmic support.

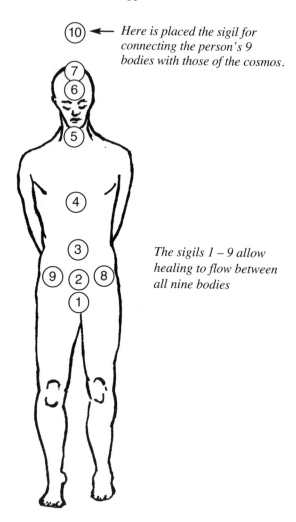

*Here is placed the sigil for
connecting the person's 9
bodies with those of the cosmos.*

*The sigils 1 – 9 allow
healing to flow between
all nine bodies*

These sigils enable healing to occur in the upper bodies of all
life. This helps erase patterns from past-life memories that
interfere with healing of the four lower bodies.

(Figure 93)

Belvaspata Sigils

These can be used by Master and Grand Master practitioners

1.
Sigil to Achieve the Optimum Ph
of the Blood *(alkaline/acidity ratio)*

Kerenech-vravi-hereshvivasta   Angel: *Klubechspi-klanavek*

2.
Sigil for the Fetus of an Unborn Infant

Gershta-uklechva-heresvik   Angel: *Pelevik-ustetvi-hereskla*

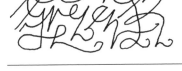

3.
Sigil for the Reptilian Brain

Kereshbrikbranavitspaha   Angel: *Kluastragnesvi*

4.
Sigil for the Medulla

Kleshvi-stauherespi   Angel: *Klachvi-meshpi*

(Figure 94)

267

5.

Sigils for the Limbic Brain
(helps magnetic/electrical harmony)
Use all of the below for addictions

a.

Kluagna-uvestrava   Angel: *Pereheretruavar*

b.

Perspratnahut-ulu-echblavaa   Angel: *Septiveravaar*

c.

Kluabresbistuvanar   Angel: *Setvikleshvrahaar*

6.

Sigil for the Amygdala

Kersvravigraniksteravi   Angel: *Erekherashvi-krechvi*

(Figure 95)

Belvaspata Sigils

7.   *Sigils for the Neo-Cortex*

a.

Birharnavaksetvravish   Angel: *Eravasvetvi*

b.

Granigverevishvahet   Angel: *Gelvishvrasbi*

8.   *Sigil for the Spinal Cord*

Kranighereshnutvavi   Angel: *Kregnish-herespa*

9.   *Sigil for Cerebrospinal Fluid*

Kritvrapeleshvihasvrabi   Angel: *Kru-anegvashpavi*

(Figure 96)

269

Belvaspata Sigils

10.

Sigil for the Pons

Kelstra-hurva-ukluaverespi

Angel: *Ilistrava-klubaberesbi*

11.

Sigil for the Cognitive Heart Center

Kerenastravaa-heshbi

Angel: *Kelstri-uklechvarvaa*

12.

Sigil for the Cognitive Stomach Center
(the 'gut' feeling, or instinct)

Kersstabaahershvi

Angel: *Kluagnetvrichvravi*

13.

Sigil for the Corpus Callosum
Connecting the Left & Right Brain Hemispheres

Birnik-hevrasta-kregnig

Angel: *Pilnikhershvrata*

(Figure 97)

Belvaspata Sigils

14.   *Sigil for the Cerebellum*

Pelvisprespata-uhurivesbi-kleshvrataa   Angel: *Kliugnesvi-beleshta*

---

15.   *Sigil for the Centrum*

Krechvaa-erstu-helesvaa   Angel: *Bilich-hestvik-neshvaa*

---

16.   *Sigil for 12 Cranial Nerves*

Kirnit-pleplastavi   Angel: *Hereshvabluavet*

---

17.   *Sigil for Reticular Alarm Activation System*
(helpful for hyperactive children)

Kelhasbraseluvitbareshta   Angel: *Pritlaresuit*

---

18.   *Sigil for Vagus System*

Kelavabra-ushvabistaunag   Angel: *Belaviranachtravi*

(Figure 98)

Questions and Answers About Belvaspata

Q. Does one have to be initiated to use the sigils and if so, how?

A. Absolutely. If one were to ask an initiate, they will be able to describe just how profound the initiation experience is as the sigils are conveyed from a master healer's hands.

There are two ways to get the initiations: Firstly, there is a Belvaspata website that lists master healers. If enough students contact a healer to make it worth their while to travel to a specific area, initiations can be performed there.

Secondly, Belvaspata initiations can be done by oneself under the long-distance guidance of a master practitioner. Students should prepare by spending a day internalizing the 12 pairs of emotions for Level I and the 16 rays of light for Level II, for example.

Q. With the new laws of attraction, light attracts opposites. Doesn't this mean light workers will be surrounded by those in illusion?

A. No, because the Goddess has written into the Book of Life that heart energy will be the most dominant factor in this new cycle, so that opposite energies repel and same energies attract.

Q. Please explain why in the master initiation the chakra 10" above the head is done last and out of order.

A. The Lemurian name for 'ten' is 'Lahun'. This means one in all and all in one. The 'law of the one' the Atlantean mysteries taught about, also pertains to the mystical principles of the 10th chakra:

As an initiate[98] becomes an adept and later a master (all three of these phases are still in Ego-Identification) 12 chakras open. During subsequent evolutionary stages such as God-Consciousness and Ascended Mastery, the tenth chakra (about the size of a dinner plate often depicted as a sign of enlightenment above the head in Egyptian and Sumerian art), 10" above the head, enlarges. It continues to grow bigger and bigger until it encloses all other chakras during the

98. See The Stages of Man in *Secrets of the Hidden Realms*.

Ascended Mastery stage. All is now in one, and one is in all. By initiating it last, this process is activated.

Q. If we accept payment for this sacred healing modality, aren't we blocking the flow of supply?

A. Every time a first or second level healer uses the sigils, a portion of the Earth and its population is healed. Because the master sigil connects the master healer to the cosmic grid, every time a master healer heals with these sigils, it effects the cosmos. How can any amount of money ever be adequate repayment? You will still be leaving the cosmos in your debt.

Q. How was this healing modality received by you?

A. I was explaining to a healer in my class in Ireland why her energy-based modality wouldn't work, when I saw a group of butterflies come through the windows and turn into symbols as they flew over her right shoulder. They flew into my forehead. I ran to the board and started writing the symbols and accompanying words as rapidly as I could.

Class ended at that point; but in my hotel room the sigils, words and information came through the night until 7am the next morning.

Appendix I

The Legend of Princess Scotia in Ireland
Written by the Master Joe of the Order of the White Rose

Princess Scotia was the daughter of Merytaten, who herself was the daughter of Nefertiti and the Pharaoh Amenhotep IV. He was also known as Akenaten. Akenaten was later to become known as Moses. Princess Scotia was married to Niul of Scythia. Both Princess Scotia and Niul journeyed to Ireland via Spain.

Ireland in earlier times was known as Scotia long before it was known as Hibernia and long before Scotland took its name from Scotia also.

Clonmacnoise is a high energy site as many ley lines criss-cross through it. Originally an ancient druid and pagan site, which became a Christian monastic site founded by Saint Ciaran in 545 AD. It is located in the county of Offaly on the river Shannon, Ireland's longest river. Christian churches were known to be built on ancient pagan sites, not by accident, as the early Christian Church Leaders knew the high energy produced by these sites. This was as a result of the ley lines intersecting at these locations. Today Clonmacnoise is an important recognized monastic site. It is the burial ground for thirteen High Kings of Ireland, a place of high energy and has an association with magical and mystical powers. There are many limestone boulders located here and one of them is known as Fairy's or Horseman's Stone. Many crosses are engraved on it and it also has the shape of a footprint embedded in it.

A fragment of stone engraved with the Flower of Life, an artifact from the monastic site, can be viewed on one of the walls in the Interpretive Center in Clonmacnoise. The same Flower of Life symbols can also be found on the walls in many of the temples in Egypt today. This gives a clear indication of the direct connection between Egypt and Clonmacnoise. Clonmacnoise has been used by many cultures and religions. During Pope John Paul II's visit to Ireland, he celebrated Mass at the site, indicating the importance that was placed on the monastic site.

This is where the time tunnel was that had the direct connection back to Egypt.

During the weekend of the 28th and 29th of January, 2006, a group of people gathered at the healing center alongside the monastic site at Ard na Rí. This weekend was to usher in the Divine Feminine back onto the planet. Over the course of the weekend the time tunnel was located again and, following a ceremony, was closed by Isis. This was to fulfill an agreement, according to Isis, the group had made 4000 years earlier in Egypt.

Princess Scotia was killed in a battle near Tralee in the South of Ireland in County Kerry. The battle was fought against the Tuatha De Danann who were defeated. Afterwards, they went underground to become the fairies of Ireland, according to legend and folklore.

The battle was fought in Scotia's Glen, near Tralee and the flagstone under which she is reported to be buried, has the imprint of a foot on it. Legend has it, that this footprint was that of Scotia, left as she leaped across the glen.

Just north of Tralee is the village of Knocknagashel. This is the home of Darby O'Gill who was immortalized by Walt Disney in the movie "Darby O'Gill & the Little People." This movie tells of Darby's encounters with King Brian, the King of the Fairies.

All of these tell of a magical time and a magical land which has gone from being real to just stories, myths and legends. Thankfully with the return of the Order of the White Rose and the Cat Magic of Isis, this magical and mystical land of Ireland will once again be restored to what it once was.

Map of Ireland with Clonmacnoise

1. Dublin
2. Clonmacnoise
3. Tralee
4. Cork
5. Galway

(Figure 99)

275

Appendix II

The Power of Ytolan
(Excerpt from *Secrets of the Hidden Realms*)

During the last week of February 2005, I was called by the Dweller to the Halls of Amenti. He led me to a chamber off the channel that runs through the Earth and equates to the pranic tube in humans. In humans it is the size of one's middle finger touching one's thumb tip to tip and it runs from the crown to the base of the spine. In the Earth it runs from a location near the Great Pyramid to a point off the coast of Maui.

The Dweller (see Appendix III) showed me the key to the power of Ytolan, that sacred object that allows thoughts to materialize. It would be used in the near future by the soon-to-be Sacred Government to create beautiful and elegant living supplies for all without depleting the environment, just the way Atlantis was built.[99]

During the week that the Sacred Government for the Earth was called by the masters and the Key of the Power of Ytolan was once again seen, three men from Antares stood in the back of my classroom. They wore simple white robes and their long white hair hung down their backs. They spoke to a brother in the back of the class and said they had come just to observe. They confirmed they had come from Antares without a craft.

I have often thought about that unexpected visit from those holy ones who simply called themselves "The Three Wise Ones, Separate Yet One". Could we have attracted their attention because the handing of the Key of Ytolan to the world of men signalled that once again a noteworthy time of enlightenment had dawned on planet Earth?

One day perhaps we shall be able to ask them as humankind reaches its maturity among the star families.

Appendix III

The Nine Lords and Their Symbols
(Excerpt from *Journey to the Heart of God*)

1. Untanas—The Keeper of the Halls of the Dead. He quenches life and the right to incarnate when light or the life force is greatly diminished through resistance to life. In this way he plays his part in

---

99. Mother has restored it to the cosmic life force center and will now be using Her own power as of 2007.

the evolution of awareness. The soul or life force of man appears as floating flames of various degrees of brightness in the Halls of the Dead. When the light grows to a great luminosity, he sets that individual free from the bondage of death. He is called Lord Three.

2. **Quertas**—The one who gives life to form. As Untanas quenches life by 'swallowing' the flame with his darkness, so Quertas kindles the flame of indwelling life, called the inner fire, to bring life to form. He is the one that will gauge when humanity's light has grown bright enough to be set free from mortality. He is Lord Four.

3. **Chietal**—Holds the key to the power of intent. He is the great lord of manifestation who guards and guides the abilities of humankind to manipulate reality. Humans are endowed with abilities to manifest reality that astonish higher races. This entire holographic environment of denser material life is held in place by our minds. We daily manifest our environment but because our thoughts have tended to be chaotic, we have manifested a large degree of chaos, not realizing how powerful we are. This is monitored in a way that allows the race to fulfill its destiny and not prematurely self-destruct. Chietal is Lord Five.

4. **Goyana**—Is responsible for the initiations and the unveiling of the mysteries along a path of enlightenment. The sacred powers and keys must be guarded from the eyes of the profane, yet accessed by those who have relinquished their personal desires upon the altar of enlightenment. Many keys to knowledge are hidden in language and symbols. He is Lord Six.

5. **Huertal**—Master of space and time, he regulates the Earth's various timelines and the speed at which time passes. For example, we have come to a close of many cycles and in preparation many karmic requirements had to be met. Over the past years, time has felt as though it has sped up—two years feels like ten. But time actually slowed down in order to fit everything in before the cosmic ascension started in February 2005. In other words, time had been compressed (as in the moments before an accident when it seems like an eternity) so we can fit more into it. Every two years may have had ten years of change and hardships and growth packed into them. Huertal opens up the ability to travel through time and space to those who have mastered themselves. He is Lord Seven.

6. **Semveta**—He is the weigher of human hearts and works with timing.

The great service density brings, is that rapid growth is possible because of it and it acts as a timing mechanism. Density can either be used by the aware lightseeker to speed up progress by transmuting hardship to wisdom, or it will slow the progress of others who choose to stay on the treadmill of karma longer by failing to learn their lessons. Timing is vitally important in any evolution or else the growth will lack strength. An example is the struggle of the chicken emerging from an egg—if we pull the chicken out sooner than it would have emerged on its own, it lacks the strength to survive. Semveta is Lord Eight.

7. **Ardal**—is Lord Nine, holder of white light and the keeper of keys. The master orchestrating chaos and order, he works with humanity's destiny. He balances the unfolding of the purpose of the Infinite through individuals as well as the race into which they incarnate. He keeps chaos at bay.

8. **The Dweller**—is the planetary lord who keeps the planetary axis stable. He is instrumental in guiding the planet as a blueprint for the cosmos; the microcosm that is the way-shower of tomorrow. He ensures that the planet stays on track in its pivotal role within the big picture.

Appendix IV

The Three Ascension Attitudes
(Excerpt from *Journey to the Heart of God*)

The attitudes of love, praise and gratitude are representative of the trinity found throughout the matrix of existence. They crown a sanctified life in glory and carry man to immortality and ascension, waiting beyond his present horizon.

Love

Emerson wrote: "Alas! I know not why... each man sees over his own experience a certain stain of error, whilst that of other men looks fair and ideal."

The word love is bandied about; it streams from pulpits, across restaurant tables, in flowery cards of all descriptions. The fact is that very few philosophers have shed much light on how the love we feel in romance and the love for God and Creation can be reconciled. There is an abundance of literature which extols romantic love; yet many spiritual writings dismiss it as an unworthy reflection of infinite love.

Because romantic love is the most intoxicating feeling most humans will ever have (called by philosophers "the enchantment of human life"), it has been compounded by feelings of guilt that such intense love should instead have been given to God. In the lives of most, no love will ever again compare to the heady, runaway, romantic emotion of youth. In this quandary, we found ourselves lacking in devotion; and so tried to love God with all fervour we could muster. For many, this was a nebulous and undefined concept, often creating religious fanatics who, failing in their feelings, tried to compensate through their actions.

The very turbulence of our romantic love carves out of our souls the hollows that will hold a greater love. Through love for a father, a mother, a child, a lover, etc. our love grows to include all people.

Intense romantic love awakens within us the ability to love others more deeply; but it also awakens so much more. The depth an artist brings to art likewise stems from passion inspired by love. Eventually, not only that which we create but that which we are, gets honed and shaped into a maturity that is lacking in those who have never truly loved another.

We learn through our Earthly loves how to surrender to something greater, that one day we may merge with our own higher identity. We find through love's muse the poet within us, the spontaneity of the inner child. We know what it is like to follow our hearts and abandon reason. Love mellows us and reduces our resistance to life as we grow older; what we forfeit in intensity we gain in inclusiveness.

The heart cannot fully love while there is an internal dialog, though one can only know that retrospectively. As the mind silences, the heart bursts open with an all-encompassing melting tenderness for all life. Divine love takes its place upon the throne of the heart.

Praise

As a child, I had a fear of heights. When on the high rides of the carnival or perched in our mulberry tree, I found that I could overcome my fear by focusing on the far horizon. By slightly altering the focus of my eyes, the dizzy heights became friendlier.

Praise is an attitude that focuses on the distant vistas and allows itself to enjoy the breathtaking view. It acknowledges that there is an unpaid bill, but focuses instead on the nurturing and abundant supply that flows to one who trusts in it.

Praise is an attitude of thoughts raised heavenward, nowhere better illustrated than the story of Christ walking on the water as told in the New Testament. He did not focus on the stormy seas, but steadfastly kept his focus on indwelling life rather than form. The disciple Peter, who wished to walk on the water also, saw the billowing waves and the high winds and sank. The master had to reach forth his hand and save him. Christ lived in a state of praise, but Peter did not.

As an ascension attitude, praise needs to be tempered by experience. It is not enough to withdraw from life to spend our days singing songs of praise to God. Our highest purpose in being here is to explore the known.

There is no redundancy in the cosmos. If there is a beggar in the street, there is also the need for him to be there. It could be that a greater master has undertaken to play this role, to give us the opportunity for compassionate understanding. Whatever the reason may be, there will be ample cause for praise if we change our focus from appearances to indwelling life.

Praise fills the cells with light and our footsteps become a blessing to the Earth. All life we touch responds with increased growth to such a life affirming frequency. Filled with praise we also fill with increased light and life force.

Gratitude

If true happiness lies in being happy with what we have, rather than being happy when we get what we want, gratitude is the key to happiness. It helps us value the little joys of the moment rather than wait for the large windfalls, and in doing so we learn to appreciate life.

Life consists of the small treasures like the quiet oasis of the undisturbed moment with a cup of tea that allows us to return to the inner world of contemplation. We can turn the weary tread of drudgery into a lightened gait with gratitude. The cherishing warmth of a favourite quilt on a dark, rain-drenched night; the moment of feeling the coming of spring in the air; the rosy cheeked pleasure of rocking a little child to sleep, eyelids weighted by the adventures of her day; all these treasured moments through awareness become ample reason for a heart to brim with gratitude.

Not only does gratitude bless us with joy, but also with increase. One of the most concealed laws of supply is that gratitude opens the floodgates of heaven, increasing anything it focuses on. Would we wish to increase our health, our abundance and our abilities? Then the place to begin is in grateful acknowledgement of whatever we already have. Let us focus in appreciation and joy on how much it means to have it. With each dollar we spend with sincere, heartfelt gratitude, many more will find their way into our pocket.

Like the other ascension attitudes, gratitude is life affirming to all whom it contacts. Indigenous peoples have always known that nature responds favorably to gratitude; that species thrive and evolve under the grateful recognition of man. Gratitude sanctifies not only the giver, but also the recipient.

Inclusiveness demands that gratitude must not deem one as worthy and another as not worthy; but like the sun or the life-giving rain, gratitude must shed its radiance on pain and pleasure alike. It takes in-depth insight to probe behind the appearances and extract the eternal truth that Mother sends nothing but goodness.

Appendix V

The Seven Supporting Attitudes
(Excerpt from *Journey to the Heart of God*)

Time

Our lives hinge on the moment. One key event or insight can alter the course of a life forever, pivoting destiny into an entirely different direction. With it the outcome of events in the cosmos could pivot also. If, for just this moment, we can see ourselves as being the center of the cosmos, as having the ability to influence with the quality of our thoughts the very fabric of existence, what would we contribute? If we can see ourselves as this central point of influence affecting all of existence, for even one second, then we can do so for the next and the next. Then suddenly without even realizing, at some point we will discover that we have transfigured ourselves into a being of great light through the power of our thoughts, a being that has power over death and a love so great that through grace it melts the illusion of others.

Failing Successfully

A day without failure is a day without growth. Our battle in life is not against outside circumstances. After all, one strengthens that which one opposes. The true battle of a light promoter is against illusion. Every encounter with opposition is a chance to pierce the illusion and find the hidden perception. In that case, how can we really ever fail?

The most common mistake made when confronted with a challenge is to measure it against past experience. This leads us to believe we have it identified and labelled. There are four steps to help us avoid strengthening old belief systems and failing to grasp the insights.

1. We do not back away from a challenge if it is ours to tackle. We remind ourselves of the covenant we made with the Infinite to find understanding through our experiences. Therefore, we embrace a challenge if it is ours.
2. We know there is more to this challenge than just its initial appearance. We take time to see behind the appearances, because we are ever mindful that what we have undertaken to solve is uniquely ours. It can not be compared to anything anyone else has ever experienced.
3. We remind ourselves that we are really working on our destiny. Our destiny is to solve that portion of the mystery of the Infinite's Being for which we took sole responsibility. When we do this, failure versus success becomes meaningless. The only failure in the true meaning of the word, is failure to learn.
4. We realize that we created this challenge. We did so by carefully manifesting outside circumstances to learn our next insight. The solution has to benefit the growth of all.

The Attitude of Grace

The attitude of living with grace is a composite of various factors that blend into one admirable quality, inspiring to observe and imperative to cultivate, for higher consciousness awaits the one who does.

Impeccable timing is the side effect of a life of grace. There is a moment to act and a moment to cease. There is a moment to advance and a moment to retreat, often indicated by signs in our environment.

The other key component of grace is fluidity. The fluid being does not bring the last moment into the present. The past becomes a ball and chain if we drag it into the future.

The Majesty of Poise

The calm poise detected in masters of power is the culmination of a lifetime of discipline and the unconditional surrender to the unfolding of life. It is the crowning glory of a life well lived—a life in which the larger vision was the determining factor rather than a focus on the vicissitudes of every day life.

Self-Reliance

Great gains in self-reliance have been made during the last 25 to 30 years, in large part as a result of an escalating destructuring of family life. Both men and women have been plunged into single-parent units where they have had to play many roles and often find the only nurturing afforded them will have to be self-nurturing. In addition, no one can advise us on a course of action, since every individual's challenges are unique. Suddenly one day we realize that our being is our sustenance. Such a realization is the very foundation of self-reliance

Reverence

Reverence stems from the ability to glimpse the divine within form. If there are parts of Creation we exclude from our reverence, let us look a little deeper and there too we can find abundant reasons for seeing the perfection of indwelling life. It is often easier to feel reverence for nature, or the genius reflected in the works of man's hands, than for our fellow man. Reverence leaves the mark of refinement upon the one who makes it a way of life. The answer to pollution, poverty and homelessness is not more technology; it is reverence for the purposes of indwelling life in order to co-operate with it.

Generosity

If there is one thing that characterizes nature perhaps more than anything else, it is abundance. Generosity is the allowing of this natural abundance to use us as a vehicle. It is therefore simply life giving to itself. The minute we close ourselves to the flow of life, we not only close ourselves to giving, but also to receiving, and stagnation and atrophy occurs.

When all outer petals have activated their frequencies by our living their corresponding attitudes, the central portal of Ara-ka-na opens within our DNA. This great event signals that we have moved to the next level in the evolution of consciousness.

Appendix VI

Man's Sexual and Social Developmental Stages
(Excerpt from *Journey to the Heart of God*)

Understanding the four bands of compassion found within the Infinite and its Creation is a bit like discovering the Fibonacci sequence for the first time. Once you know it, it suddenly becomes apparent in life's expressions all around you. The four bands of compassion will be found to provide the pattern for evolving life everywhere, from conflict resolution, social and relationship stages to sexual development. *(See Fig. 101)*

The sexual stages of man pertain to the way the opposite sexes relate to one another and move through the bands of compassion from the top (as illustrated) to the bottom during identity consciousness. Immediately preceding God-consciousness they move from the bottom to the top, symbolizing the blue road home.

In the current industrialized societies these natural developmental stages have been severely disrupted by the corruption from the media, the increase of neglect and child abuse resulting from the destruction of primary family units. When societies are declining or destructuring, this becomes the case. *(See Fig. 100)*

1. Seeking Sameness: (Pre-adolescence)

During pre-adolescence boys and girls gravitate towards same sex groups in order to learn more about what it means to be a boy or a girl by observing it in their same sex peers. Boys build "Girls Keep Out" clubhouses and girls often view boys as the 'enemy' as they huddle together in giggling groups. If sexual activity does occur, it usually involves same-sex masturbation or exploration of the self through self-masturbation.

2. Seeking Sameness With Interest in the Opposite: (Adolescence)

While remaining in the safety of the same-sex peer groups, adolescents now develop an obsessive interest in the opposite sex. During this stage the quest to understand their own sexuality continues but with increasing curiosity about the opposite sex.

Boys spend hours lifting weights, considering cars to drive when they get old enough to have a license and other "manly" pursuits that are culturally appropriate. It is a time of proving themselves as "a man." Hours are spent studying and obsessively speculating about the opposite sex.

Girls spend a great deal of time with their same-sex peers learning to become "a woman." They study magazines, makeup, fashion. They worry endlessly about their bodies and appearance, fed by the unrealistic portrayal of the feminine ideal the media gives. They speculate in groups about the opposite sex. Generally, if sex does occur with the opposite sex, they retreat back into the same-sex group as their main support group after the encounter.

3. Understanding the Opposite by Experiencing it Within the Familiar: (Late teens, early twenties)

Cliques or groups of both sexes with similar interests form so that they may study each other in the safety of the group. Sororities, the "jocks" and cheerleaders, the intellectuals, the rebels and other groups with similar characteristics form.

Sexual encounters can now be explored with one another within the safety of a support group with similar values. At a time when they are still unsure about their sexuality, their peers mirror to them that they are acceptable (unfortunately a similar reason forms the basis of many friendships).

The sexual relationships are superficial during this stage. They are not interested in the deep exploration of the emotions or minds of their partners but rather in broadening their experience.

4. Experiencing the Opposite: (Mid-twenties and later)

During the mid-twenties and later, isolated relationships form and the association with peer groups becomes more peripheral. The opposite sex is now studied in depth as we search to understand our own inner opposite gender through our partners. The emotions and thoughts of partners become as important as the physical aspects of the relationship.

Appendix VII

Transfiguring into a God-Being in the Flesh
(Excerpt from *Secrets of the Hidden Realms*)

The evolution of a human being into the stage that lies beyond humanness, that of a god-being that can come and go throughout the cosmos with the speed of thought, follows three distinct stages. Each stage has within it three separate phases. This brings the total number of phases to nine through which a human being can evolve.

Stage 1. Identity Consciousness

This stage is like the bottom of the pyramid in that many enter this stage but far fewer make it through. The three phases of this stage are all lived while in ego-identification, that state of beingness that sees ourselves as separate from others and identifies with the body and surface mind (the ego).

Phase 1. The Initiate

Type of Change: Transformation. Transformation is the stage within change that discards that which is no longer needed. The truth seeker dies to the old way of being.

Four Great Bands of Compassion

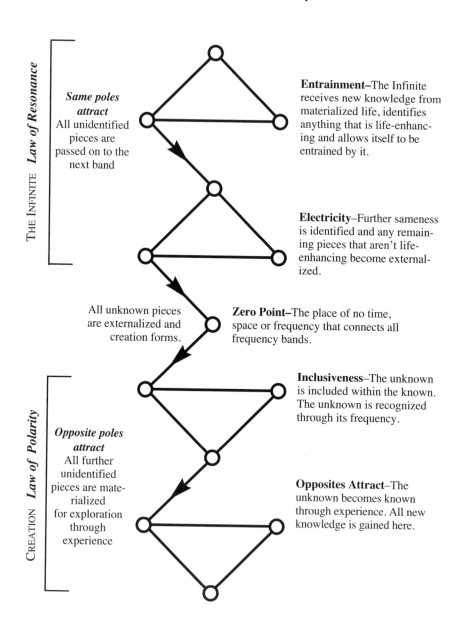

Same poles attract
All unidentified pieces are passed on to the next band

Entrainment–The Infinite receives new knowledge from materialized life, identifies anything that is life-enhancing and allows itself to be entrained by it.

Electricity–Further sameness is identified and any remaining pieces that aren't life-enhancing become externalized.

All unknown pieces are externalized and creation forms.

Zero Point–The place of no time, space or frequency that connects all frequency bands.

Inclusiveness–The unknown is included within the known. The unknown is recognized through its frequency.

Opposite poles attract
All further unidentified pieces are materialized for exploration through experience

Opposites Attract–The unknown becomes known through experience. All new knowledge is gained here.

THE INFINITE *Law of Resonance*

CREATION *Law of Polarity*

These four frequency bands form the matrix and offer all evolving life.
By aligning with them, we draw upon the power of the All.

(Figure 100)

286

Sexual Stages of Mankind

GOD-CONSCIOUSNESS *(Stages evolve this way)*

IDENTITY CONSCIOUSNESS *(Stages evolve this way)*

4. Seeking Only Sameness– During the final stage of human evolution, one only identifies with indwelling life and not form. Another is seen as a door to eternity.

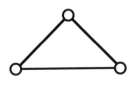

1. Seeking Sameness– Pre-adolescence. Boys and girls seek same-sex play-mates. This strengthens sexual identity.

3. Examining Humanness within Oneness– We re-enter the human condition even though we remember our oneness. If it is conducive to growth, we may choose to engage in sex.

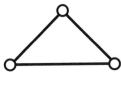

2. Seeking Sameness *(with intense interest in opposite sex)*– Early-adolescence. Boys and girls each participate in same-sex activities but obsess about the opposite sex.

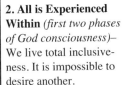

2. All is Experienced Within *(first two phases of God consciousness)*– We live total inclusiveness. It is impossible to desire another.

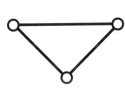

3. Understanding the Opposite *(by experiencing it within the familiar)*– Late teens and early twenties. Boys and girls experience the opposite sex within groups of combined sexes. The relationships are more superficial.

1. Opposites Merge *(pre-ceding entry into God consciousness)*– The masculine and feminine within merge to give birth to the God-being. Sexual desires decline.

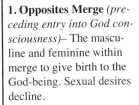

4. Experiencing the Opposite– Mid-twenties and later. In-depth and iso-lated relationships form with mental/emotional exploration. We get to know our own opposite sex within by studying it in another.

Understanding these stages can aid us in honoring where we and others are along the path of unfoldment in human sexuality.

(Figure 101)

Testing: Fear. To have all belief systems, identities and worldviews eradicated, leaves one without the comfort of shelters or a frame of reference and creates fear.

Changes: The seals of debris in the chakras start to burst open, causing at times physical distress in their areas. The chakras become spherical, instead of resembling a cone to the front and a cone to the back with the narrow ends meeting in the middle.

Challenges: The Initiate has to learn not to take anything at face value but to cultivate the necessary humility that will remind him for the rest of his journey that all he can know for certain is that he doesn't know.

Phase 2. The Adept

Type of Change: Transmutation. During transmutation something of a lower frequency is changed into another substance of a higher frequency, much like the alchemist changing lead to gold. In this instance, challenge is transmuted to insight.

Testing: Addiction. Every stage's second phase has the testing of addiction. In this phase the adept learns how to turn challenges into power by seeing behind the appearances of 'problems.' This results in power surges that create endocrine releases of hormones that can be very addictive. The adept can become addicted to challenge.

Changes: As the adept learns to cooperate with the challenges of life, every challenge becomes a source of power and energy; this causes the spherical chakras to become enlarged and overlap each other more and more.

Challenge: The adept can take himself too seriously at this point and so divert his attention from chasing challenges to balancing the sub-personalities. It is essential to become emotionally self-reliant at this point by bringing balance and expression to our inner family. If we neglect this, it is unlikely that we will pass the testing of power presented during the next phase.

Phase 3. The Master

Type of Change: Transfiguration. The third phase of every stage tests us with power. Because it is seeing whether we are worthy of the major evolutionary leap that occurs during transition from stage to stage, its testing is severe. Passing the test produces transfiguration of either the fields of the body or the body itself.

Testing: Power. The master's abilities become quite apparent at this point, bringing praise and in some instances, worship from others. The feeling of power can produce a sense of gratification that can divert the master from being a perception seeker to becoming a power seeker, in which case he cannot proceed any further on the path.

Changes: Not only is power the result of bringing order to the mind, but also of the chakra spheres growing so enlarged that they form one large unified chakra field around the body. A heartache, an orgasm or the opening of the crown chakra by a peak spiritual experience, is felt throughout the body.

Challenge: At the very moment that our egos want to assert themselves, we must not waver for an instant from reaching beyond the allure of the magical world of the unknown to the far distant horizon of the unknowable. Resisting the temptations to do miracles for show, we must keep our goal of increased perception firmly in mind. Not many truth seekers make it beyond this point.

Stage 2. God Consciousness

The previous stage believed the character we play on the stage of life to be real. This stage no longer identifies with the character. In fact, during the first two phases we walk off the stage of life only to return for the third phase. But even as we again stay in character, we know without a doubt that we are just enacting a role.

Phase 1. Emptiness

Type of Change: Transformation. Everything we thought we knew gets thrown out of the window. All we know is that we are nothing. The usual emotions are gone, from the dramatic shift in perception as our minds become empty. Nothing in our lives makes sense anymore and a great disassociativeness is felt.

Testing: Fear. Although the testing in the first phase of every stage is fear, most ordinary, everyday fears were overcome during the previous stage. Now the very foundation upon which we have stood has been knocked out from underneath us. Not only do we at times feel terrified, but a vast loneliness grips us. We feel afraid when expanding too much, fearing we may lose our self-awareness just as we have lost our identities; afraid that our responsibilities won't be properly done. But something larger is running our lives and everything gets done without much forethought. We feel claustrophobic when we contract our awareness back into the body.

Changes: The changes that take place during this entire stage affect the emotional body. During this phase the emotional body forms a large round ball, slightly larger than the luminous cocoon formed by the seven bodies of man under usual circumstances.

Challenge: If enough fear is present, one can step out of God-consciousness and, because one didn't stay in long enough to enjoy the more blissful states that come later, be hesitant to try it again. This could then keep us locked into Identity-Consciousness. It is helpful to have someone ahead on the path be able to say that the disassociativeness one is experiencing is appropriate to this rather bewildering phase.

Phase 2. The Bliss

Type of Change: Transmutation. The realization that it is not that we are nothing, it's that we are all things, transmutes the feeling of complete emptiness to the fullness of bliss. We feel everything as though it is inside us.

Testing: Addiction. The test is a difficult one, not only because of its intense addictive quality, but because most traditions teach that this is the end goal of the spiritual seeker's path. The years of disciplined living have to somehow penetrate the euphoria and remind us that there is no point of arrival.

Changes: A strange phenomenon now takes place in the emotional field, reducing the physical energy, while creating a vastness of emotion. It is as though the desire of the cosmos has become one's own. The emotional body forms rope-like spikes radiating out from the physical body. When I first observed this in my own field, I thought that the shock of encountering the Infinite's vastness had shredded my emotional body. Only later did I realize that it was an appropriate part of the bliss phase.

Challenge: There is very little growth during the first two phases of God-consciousness when one essentially walks off the stage of life. The master has no boundaries and is in a very vulnerable state. But because others around him are allowed to misbehave as they choose, they aren't growing either. The great challenge of this phase is to remember that there is value to the play; that it was designed that all may grow. The master has to re-enter the human drama while remembering it's just a play.

Phase 3. Re-Entering the Human Condition

Type of Change: Transfiguration. The emotional body now expands itself to twice its former size, completely transfiguring the size of the body's luminous cocoon.

Testing: As with all third phases, the testing concerns the impeccable use of power. The master has the ability to manifest whatever he or she wants to, but having spent many years gathering such power, must now forgo using it in most instances in favor of cooperating fully with life.

Changes: The changes that occur during this phase create intense emotion. But even as the renewed emotions again churn the surface of the master's life, the vast stillness of expanded awareness lies beneath.

Challenge: The tremendous power that is part of the master's life at this point demands the utmost respect and sensitivity for all lifeforms. It also requires the master's full cooperation in order to become a tool in providing learning opportunities for others. In other words, the master becomes a steward of all life.

Stage 3. Ascended Mastery

The three stages themselves follow the roadmap of all change: Transformation, Transmutation, Transfiguration. The stage of **Identity-consciousness** is in essence transformational in that it is the shedding of that which no longer serves, namely the ego.

The **God-consciousness stage** is transmutational in that it turns a form of awareness that learns very little from experience, into a combination that does. In its third phase the master observes his experiences from an eternal perspective while again enacting the human drama—it feels a lot like thinking with two minds at once.

The **Ascended Mastery stage** transfigures not only the fields of the body, as do the other two stages, but also the physical body itself. To transfigure something that dense is a tremendous accomplishment and the primary function of this stage is transfiguration.

Phase 1. The Totally Silent Mind

Type of Change: Transformational. Previous God-consciousness phases had silence within the mind during any time the master did not have to relate or act. Now, even this form of inner dialog is discarded. Interaction, writing, speaking is done from a place of complete silence as though being on 'auto-pilot'. The silence is only broken occasionally to do something deductive.

Testing: Fear. It takes a lot of trust to have your mouth speak that which you didn't first think of. If anything is done from a place of old, obsolete programming, everything starts to spin. One is physically incapable of doing something that is not meant to be. The overall fear is that life is completely out of control and it is—out of the control of the egoic self. But the vast cosmic mind governs our lives at this point.

Changes: Because of the transfigurative qualities of this entire stage, every phase has very dramatic changes, all of them pertaining to the mental or linear bodies of man. In this phase the mental body implodes into a pinpoint of light, pulling the emotional body with it. It then explodes and fuses with the etheric body. The emotional body becomes smaller and denser.

Challenge: The vestiges of a desire for a personal life have to be laid aside at this point. The master can and must make sure that his life has joy and balance in it. His life affects too much to have it be anything less. But his life's work is pre-determined by his contract with the Infinite. To a certain extent, he can determine how he wishes the work to unfold, but he cannot deviate from his purpose. He cannot allow the total inner silence to seduce him into inaction.

Phase 2. Immortality

Type of Change: Transmutation. This is the incredible phase in which mortal matter is transmuted into immortal matter—'lead is turned into gold.' The whole event takes but minutes to complete and feels like a lightning flash throughout the body.

Testing: The bliss that follows this transmutation far exceeds what was experienced before. Within the body of the Immortal Master, the energy lines zig-zag through the areas where the chakras used to be localized. In women they criss-cross from side to side and in men from front to back. They end in the area above the pineal gland, about four inches apart, and excrete a substance that is the hormone for this level of bliss (also called the life hormone). It can be tasted as a sweet substance in the back of the palate during intense bliss. Once again, addiction becomes the challenge.

Changes: The Immortal Mastery phase culminates in yet another spectacular alteration in the bodies of man. The spiritual mental body implodes to a pinprick of light and when it explodes, merges with the combined mental/etheric bodies and carries them outward, forming a large sphere around the body. The emotional bodies fill the sphere and the spirit body's light-fibers radiate out from the life force center through the sphere.

Challenge: The unseen realms present an alluring detour during the third phase of Identity-consciousness. Yet now they become a way of life. They are no longer seen by the master to be outside himself, so no longer present an enticement in the former way. But beings from the various unseen kingdoms we dwell amongst are attracted to the master's light and enter his life. The master has to learn to know the many different idiosyncrasies of dealing with the various beings around him so that he can further refine his ability to benefit all life. This helps him resist the temptation of inactivity induced by bliss.

Phase 3. Life More Abundant

Type of Change. Transfiguration The change that occurs with this transfiguration is the apex of human achievement; it creates an evolutionary leap that only nine Ascended Masters had made up until August 2005. When fully transfigured, the master exits the human kingdom and enters the God-Kingdom.

Changes: The life force center explodes during this phase, forming a large ball of life force, slightly larger than the sphere of mental bodies. The spirit body's light fibers cluster into one rope extending from the assemblage point behind the shoulder blades, to the zero point portal that has formed behind the belly-button.

Testing: We can surmise by looking at the third phases of the previous two stages that this stage's third phase also has something to do with power. The challenge here is to accumulate, harness and conserve enough power to shatter the glass-like shield that separates kingdoms. The master has to overcome the huge temptation of over-polarizing into the light; into the seasonless place of no emotion and great peace—the place of ultimate stagnation and inaction.

Challenge: Ascended Masters have great perception. The greater our perception, the greater our emotions have to be. When emotions aren't recognized and utilized as the growth mechanisms they are, these very large emotions can be deliberately disconnected in order to experience the peace of the bliss that plays through every cell at this point. But it is the power of emotion that will crack the 'glass' shield the master has to go through to get to the next kingdom. All chakras must be participating in creating this emotional response. Most Ascended Masters live only in the upper chakras. It becomes necessary to reawaken the lower chakras, reactivate the sex drive and use it to arouse the other emotions. With the power of emotion, the shield shatters, the zero point opening explodes to fill all the fields. The fields around the body explode to double their size.

The chord of light fibers now elongates and loops from the assemblage point on the outside edge of the fields to the heart center and back again to the assemblage point. The master has become a god-being in the flesh.

The God-Kingdom—Future Destiny Of Man

A large leap of consciousness awaits man if he wishes to go beyond human boundaries. Only nine made it across this boundary before 2005.

Unlike the three stages within the human kingdom, the God-Kingdom has two levels. It is essential that more and more humans enter the God-kingdom, because it is their destiny to change the inactivity found there. Humans are accustomed to struggle, and a great struggle awaits in the God-Kingdom to avoid succumbing to the inactivity and lack of growth in that realm. The struggle is against the huge enticement of bliss. Although we encounter bliss as a testing within the human stages, the bliss of this higher stage is eight times stronger. It becomes difficult to move even a limb and activity tends to slow almost to a standstill.

During the first phase of the God-Kingdom, the fields around the body are very enlarged. The small zero point opening found behind the belly-button of an Ascended Master explodes as the transition to the God-Kingdom is made. The zero point enlarges to fill the entire mental body, pushing the emotional body outside of the mental body.

The mental body (the sum total of all the mental bodies initially found in man, fused into one) starts to rotate. The chord of light fibers loops from the assemblage point through the heart and back again. During this phase emotions are felt much more intensely.

One of the main reasons the vast majority of Ascended Masters never enter here is because it requires pulsing the emotions between their positive and negative poles, fueled by sexuality, to break the glass-like membrane between the kingdoms—something shunned by Ascended Masters until recently.

The second phase of the God-Kingdom is precipitated by yet another zero point explosion that pushes the mental body outside of the emotional body. The end result is a thin emotional body just inside the mental body, while the rest of the space is filled with the zero point. The clockwise and counter-clockwise movements of the mental body no longer make 360-degree rotations, but flip back and forth with just partial rotations. The chord of light fibers has to elongate to reach in a loop from the heart to the assemblage point on the enlarged mental body. Emotions dramatically diminish.

Other books by Almine

A Life of Miracles
Mystical Keys to Ascension
This book is deeply inspiring and motivational in its content. It is unique in its field in making man's relationship as the microcosm to the macrocosm understandable to both beginning and advanced readers. It's a detailed guide to living a joyous and balanced life and provides a carefully laid out map to achieving the magnificent destiny that beckons at the apex of human experience: ascension.

Published: 2002, 248 pages, soft cover, 6 x 9, ISBN: 978-0-972433-10-5

Journey to the Heart of God
Mystical Keys to Immortal Mastery
Ground-breaking cosmology revealed for the first time, sheds new light on previous bodies of information such as the Torah, the I Ching and the Mayan Zolkien. The explanation of man's relationship as the microcosm as set out in the previous book *A Life of Miracles*, is expanded in a way never before addressed by New Age authors, giving new meaning and purpose to human life. Endorsed by an Astro-physicist from Cambridge University and a former NASA scientist, this book is foundational for readers at all levels of spiritual growth.

Published: 2005, 276 pages, soft cover, 6 x 9, ISBN: 978-0-972433-12-9

Secrets Of The Hidden Realms
Mystical Keys to the Unseen Worlds
This remarkable book delves into mysteries few mystics have ever revealed. It gives in detail: *The practical application of the goddess mysteries • Secrets of the angelic realms • The maps, alphabets, numerical systems of Lemuria, Atlantis, and the Inner Earth • The Atlantean calender, accurate within 5 minutes • The alphabet of the Akashic libraries. Secrets of the Hidden Realms* is a truly amazing bridge across the chasm that has separated humanity for eons from unseen realms.

Published: 2006, 395 pages, soft cover, 6 x 9, ISBN: 978-0-972433-13-6

Other books by Almine

The Ring of Truth *Second Edition*
Sacred Secrets of the Goddess

As man slumbers in awareness, the nature of his reality has altered forever. As one of the most profound mystics of all time, Almine explains this dramatic shift in cosmic laws that is changing life on earth irrevocably. A powerful healing modality is presented to compensate for the changes in laws of energy, healers have traditionally relied upon. The new principles of beneficial white magic and the massive changes in spiritual warriorship are meticulously explained.

Published: 2007, 256 pages, soft cover, 6 x 9, ISBN: 978-1-934070-08-6

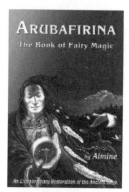

Arubafirina
The Book of Fairy Magic

This book is most certainly a milestone in the history of mysticism throughout the ages. It is the product of a rare and unprecedented event in which Almine, acknowledged as the leading mystic of our time, was granted an exceptional privilege. For one week in November 2006 she was invited to enter the fairy realms and gather the priceless information for this book. The result is a tremendous treasure trove of knowledge and interdimensional color photos.

Published: 2007, 178 pages, incl. 16 color pages, soft cover, 6 x 9, ISBN: 978-1-934070-00-0

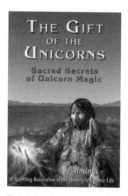

The Gift of the Unicorns
Sacred Secrets of Unicorn Magic

These life-changing insights into the deep mystical secrets of the earth's past puts the cosmic role of humanity into perspective. It gives meaning to the suffering of the ages and solutions of hope and predicts the restoration of white magic. An enlightening explanation of the causes of the Great Fall and our ascent out of ages of forgetfulness into a remembrance of our divine new purpose and oneness, is masterfully given. Truly an inspiring book!

Published: 2007, 284 pages, soft cover, 6 x 9, ISBN: 978-1-934070-01-7

Other books by Almine

Windows Into Eternity
Revelations of the Mother Goddess

The depth of insight into the ancient mysteries this book provides is without parallel. Almine, internationally renowned mystic, deftly leads the reader into the heart of the hidden laws of existence where old paradigms effortlessly fall away. These profound revelations transcend reason, delivering instead the visionary expansion readers have come to expect from this author. A metaphysical masterpiece, it delves deeply into the fascinating origins of all life and the causes of the Great Fall.

Published: 2008, soft cover, 6 x 9, ISBN: 978-1-934070-23-9

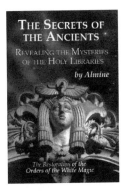

The Secrets of the Ancients
Revealing the Mysteries of the Holy Libraries

As the earth has ascended since February 2008, many mysteries have come to light to aid humanity in its rapid evolution into light. None have been as tantalizing as those revealed by the holy libraries of Earth. Long guarded by orders of incorruptible white magic, the release of these ancient libraries' information is a priceless gift to humankind. Discover the origins of illusion as found in the building blocks of reality and delve into the purposes of Creation.

Published: 2009, soft cover, 6 x 9, ISBN: 978-1-934070-37-8

Order books by phone 502-499-0016 or
*on our web site **www.spiritualjourneys.com***
Spiritual Journeys, P.O. Box 300, Newport, Oregon 97365

Wholesale: www.atlasbooks.com or call 1-800-BookLog

CDs by Almine

Each powerful presentation has a unique musical background unaltered as channeled from Source. Truly a work of art.

Retail:
To order CDs by phone call 502-499-0016 or visit our web site
www.spiritualjourneys.com

Wholesale:
www.atlasbooks.com, or call 1-800-BookLog

The Power of Emotion
This presentation describes emotion as an impetus to growth. It explains how emotion promotes awareness and how even "negative" emotions become great tools of enlightenment when properly used.

The Power of Silence
Few teaching methods empty the mind, but rather fill it with more information. As one who has achieved this state of silence, Almine meticulously maps out the path that leads to this state of expanded awareness.

The Power of Self-Reliance
Cultivating self-reliance is explained as resulting from balancing the sub-personalities—key components to emotional autonomy.

Mystical Keys to Manifestation
This shows how we can masterfully create truth moment by moment rather than seek it without.

Mystical Keys to Ascended Mastery
The way to overcome and transcend mortal boundaries is clearly mapped out for the sincere truth seeker.

The Power of Forgiveness
Digressing from traditional views that forgives a perceived injury, this explains the innocence of all experience. Instead of showing how to forgive a wrong, it acknowledges wholeness.